AF349314

Spanish with VICKY

Papel certificado por el Forest Stewardship Council®

Primera edición: junio de 2025
Tercera reimpresión: diciembre de 2025

Printed in Spain – Impreso en España

ISBN: 978-84-19441-35-5
Depósito legal: B-6.259-2025

Compuesto por Carol Borràs
Impreso en Gómez Aparicio, S. L.
Casarrubuelos (Madrid)

CM 41355

VICTORIA CH

STOP BEING A GUIRI AND FINALLY LEARN ESPAÑOL

Con ilustraciones de
MARTA PIEDRA

Random

ÍNDICE

LET'S START WITH THE BASICS

WHO ARE YOU?
MARK THE STATEMENTS YOU AGREE WITH

- ☐ Every time I say one word in Spanish, native speakers immediately switch to English.

- ☐ I get bored as soon as I open a traditional grammar book.

- ☐ I think I'm too old to learn Spanish.

- ☐ I'm tired of being treated like a guiri.

- ☐ I believe I'm not any good at languages.

- ☐ I think Spanish people speak too fast and I can't understand anything they say.

- ☐ I like gossip and hate not being able to understand conversations.

- ☐ I'm sick of sounding like a robot in Spanish.

If you marked more than 5 statements, then this book is for you. Are you tired of being a **guiri**[1] and having Spaniards switch to English the moment you say your first sentence in Spanish? Do you wonder why they do that? Maybe you've been studying grammar and you think you know Spanish, but you can't follow basic conversations. Let me tell you something: **What you learned in books is not what you'll hear on the street.** With this book, you'll finally **speak Spanish naturally** and get natives to continue the conversation in Spanish, instead of switching to English every time you open your mouth.

1. A Spanish word (used with much affection —or maybe not so much)— to describe a foreigner, usually a tourist, who stands out due to their style, customs, or somewhat... peculiar enthusiasm. It's like saying: **"You're not from here, but we love you anyway (even if you wear socks with sandals)."**

I'm Vicky, your Spanish teacher from Spain. After more than 15 years of teaching Spanish, I have all the tips to help you overcome the language barrier by helping you understand our crazy language and culture.

LET'S GET STARTED. ¡VAMOS!

1

HOLA, ¿QUÉ TAL?

→ How to greet in Spain

→ How to engage in small talk

→ How to say goodbye

→ Pronunciation basics: B and V

1

Hola, guapo, ¿Cómo vas? ¿Qué te cuentas? **¿Hablas español?**
Perdón, **yo no comprendo**, mi español es no muy bueno.

HOW TO GREET IN SPAIN
GREETINGS: LOS SALUDOS

Imagina esto: You're walking down a street in Spain.
As you pass people, you're hearing non stop **¡Hola!** or **¿Qué tal?**

It sounds really welcoming but... what does each greeting really mean?
Why do some people say **¿Qué pasa?**, while others go for **¿Cómo estás?** What are the differences?

Well, **amigo mío**, welcome to one of the first (and most essential) steps in learning Spanish: **greetings**.

Whether it's a casual **Hola** (hello), a cheery **Buenos días** (good morning), or a relaxed **¿Qué tal?** (what's up?), these phrases open the door to a world of social nuances.

There are many ways to greet someone:

Hola, buenas,
¿Qué tal?
¿Cómo vas?
¿Qué te cuentas? (informal)
¿Qué es de tu vida?
¡Cuánto tiempo! *Long time no see!*
¡Cuánto tiempo sin verte!
¡Dichosos los ojos!

And if you're a girly girl like me, you'll say:

So, what should you say according to the time of day (**Buenos días**, **Buenas tardes**, **Buenas noches**)? If you're confused and can't differentiate between the crazy Spanish times of day, let me give you a tip:

Buenos días: from 6 am to 1:59 pm

Buenas tardes: from 2 pm to 8:59 pm

Buenas noches: from 9 pm to 5 am

**And if you're still confused,
just say BUENAS. This is what everyone
says all the time** ☺

GRAMMAR TIP

NOW, LET'S SEE HOW TO ANSWER THIS VERY SIMPLE QUESTION ACCORDING TO TRADITIONAL GRAMMAR BOOKS:

—Hola, ¿qué tal?
—Hola, muy bien, gracias. ¿Y tú?
—Muy bien también, gracias.

(They both blush and don't know how to continue the **awkward** conversation.)

Has this happened to you? I'm sure your answer is yes. In Spain, most of the time **Hola, ¿qué tal?** is just a way to say "Hello." Native speakers don't expect to start a conversation with it. Look how natives do that:

Hola, ¿qué tal?
Buenas, ¿cómo vas?

And that's it. No one will expect a response. You just continue on your way and everyone is happy ☺

RESPONSES ACCORDING TO YOUR ESTADO DE ÁNIMO (MOOD):

Muy bien. *Very well.*
Genial. *Awesome.*
Superbién. *Super good.*
De maravilla. *Wonderful.*

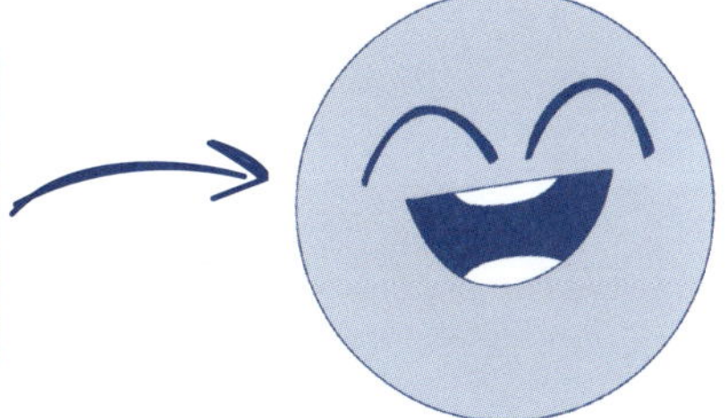

Tirando. *Getting by.*
Ahí vamos. *Hanging in there.*
No me puedo quejar. *Can't complain.*
Sin más. *So-so, nothing special.*
Sobreviviendo. *Surviving.*

Más o menos. *Pretty much.*
Bueno... *Well...*
Estaría mejor si me tocara la lotería.
    It would be better if I won the lottery.
Estoy fatal. *I'm doing awful.*
Estoy de bajón. *I'm sad.* (slang)

Want to sound like a real Spaniard?

Just use the word **hombre** when you bump into someone you know on the street!

In Spain, **hombre** means "man" but not always. It's also an expression and a way to emphasize. You can use it with men and women, because it's just an idiom that we use to:

express surprise
express disappointment
express doubt
express anger
express anything

and all that depends on the intonation!

HOW TO ENGAGE IN SMALL TALK

I'm sure you've been asked this question a thousand times, but how do you usually answer it? If you were to answer ***Mi español no es muy bueno**, let me tell you it doesn't sound natural, even if it's grammatically correct. Next time try saying:

- ✔ **Lo entiendo bastante, pero no lo hablo bien.**
  I understand it quite well, but I don't speak it very well.
- ✔ **No hablo muy bien el español.**
  I don't speak Spanish very well.
- ✔ **Todavía estoy aprendiendo.**
  I'm still learning.
- ✔ **Hablo un poco, pero me falta fluidez.**
  I speak a little, but not fluently.

FLUENCY FIX!

When speaking Spanish —or any language, really— the key is to sound natural. A lot of times, we try to translate things literally, but that doesn't always work. That's why we need to be mindful of how we use words!

For example:
Don't say **No soy fluido** when you mean "I'm not fluent." It just doesn't sound right.

Instead, say: **Me falta fluidez**, **No tengo fluidez**, or **No hablo con fluidez**.

And instead of **No comprendo**, go with **No lo entiendo**.

It sounds way more natural!

After meeting a Spanish person in Spain, the first question will probably be:

Hablas muy bien el español. ¿Cuánto hace que estás en España?

And you will probably say: ***Estoy en España PARA/POR 5 años**. However, we don't use these prepositions to express this in Spain. In some Latin American countries, they might say: **Estoy en España por 5 años**, but in Spain we say:

- ✔ **Llevo 5 meses en España.**
- ✔ **Estoy en España desde hace 5 meses.**
- ✔ **Hace 5 meses que estoy en España.**
- ✔ **Estoy en España desde 2020.**

→ **LLEVAR** + **AMOUNT OF TIME**
+ **VERBO EN GERUNDIO (-ANDO/-IENDO)**

→ **DESDE HACE** + **AMOUNT OF TIME**

→ **HACE** + **AMOUNT OF TIME**
+ **QUE** + **VERB**

To talk about the date:
DESDE + **DATE**

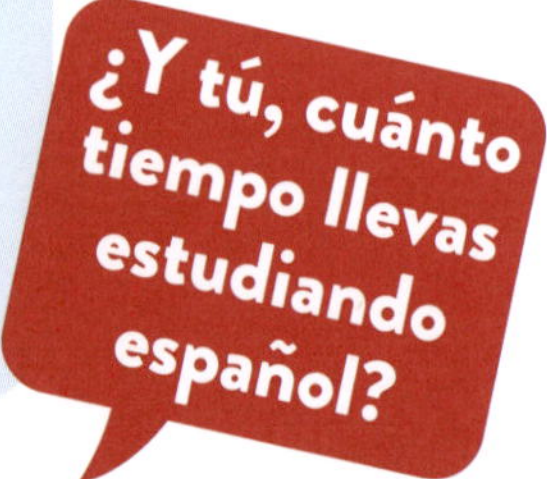

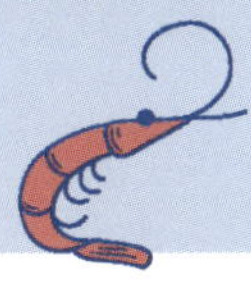

Hi, hey there! How are you? Long time no see!

Very well. Getting by, you know. And you? What's new?

Good. Working a lot, super busy.

That's good.

Totally, haha.

Well, I'm glad to see you.

Same here. Let's try to meet up soon.

Sure. Take care. All the best, and say hi to Maria for me.

Will do. Have a great weekend!

WHAT'S THE DIFFERENCE BETWEEN POCO AND UN POCO?

With uncountable nouns:
poco has a negative connotation (-)
un poco de has a positive connotation (+)

Tengo poco tiempo :(
I don't have a lot of time.

Tengo un poco de tiempo :)
I have some time.

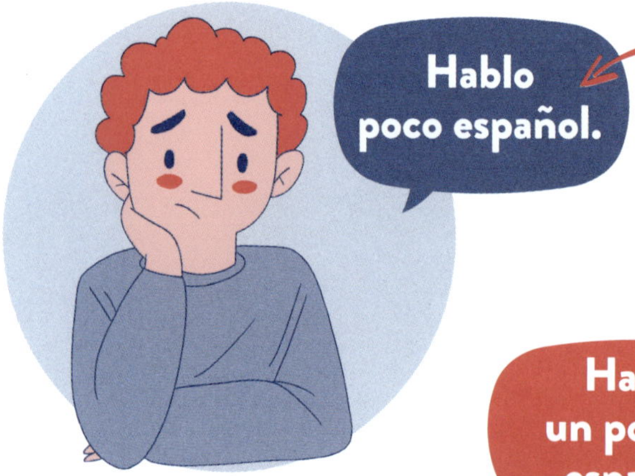

This indicates that your knowledge of Spanish is limited or basic.

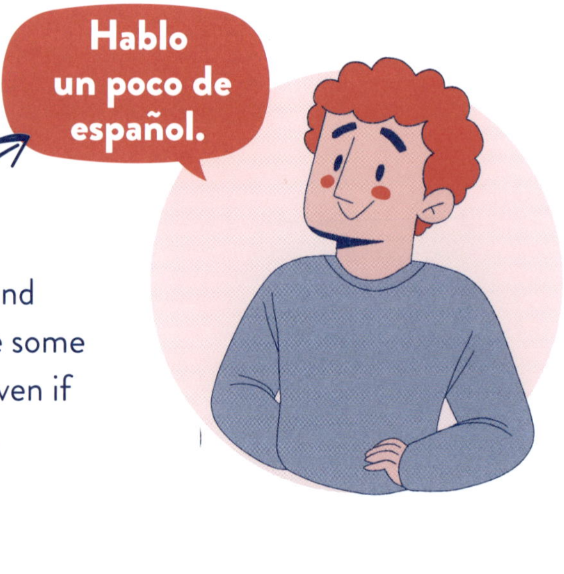

This is more positive and emphasizes that you have some knowledge of Spanish, even if you are not fluent.

HOW TO SAY GOODBYE

Now you've learned to start and engage a conversation but, what about putting an end to it? Let's learn how to end a conversation when you want to leave and be polite:

- ✔ **Bueno, me tengo que ir corriendo.**
  Well, I've got to go. I'm in a hurry.
- ✔ **Me voy, que me están esperando.**
  I'm off. Someone's waiting for me.
- ✔ **Te dejo, que tengo prisa.**
  I'll let you go. I'm in a hurry.

And my favorite:

ME VOY A IR YENDO. *I'm gonna get going.*
Yes, we use the verb **IR** three times.

Or what my mother would say:

I'm leaving because I have lentils on the stove.

To say goodbye, we use the verb **despedirse**.

Normal people (not cyborgs) say:

- ✔ **Hasta luego.** *See you later.*
- ✔ **Hasta otra.** *See you next time.*
- ✔ **Hasta mañana.** *See you tomorrow.*
- ✔ **Hasta pronto.** *See you.*
- ✔ **Nos vemos.** *See you.*
- ✔ **Ya te llamaré.** *I'll call you.*
- ✔ **Que vaya bien, cuídate.** *Take care.*
- ✔ **Me alegro de verte.** *Nice to see you.*
- ✔ **Recuerdos a tu mujer.** *Say hi to your wife for me.*
- ✔ **Hablamos pronto.** *Talk soon.*
- ✔ **Estamos en contacto.** *We'll be in touch.*

PRONUNCIATION BASICS: B AND V

Now let's answer a very common question that I'm sure you have:

ARE B AND V PRONOUNCED THE SAME?

YES! The letters b and v are pronounced the same in almost all dialects. In some regions, there may be a slight difference due to regional influences or emphasis, but this is **RARE** and not standard. **B AND V** both represent a single phoneme and their sound changes slightly depending on their position in a word or sentence. Here's an explanation:

THE TWO SOUNDS OF B AND V:

[b]:
- This is a plosive bilabial sound (the lips fully close, and then the sound is released).
- It happens at the beginning of a word or after a pause or a nasal sound like m or n.
- Examples:
  - **boca** *mouth* → ['boka]
  - **invierno** *winter* → [im'bjeɾno]

[β]:
- This is an approximant bilabial sound (the lips come close together, but don't fully close).
- It occurs between vowels or in other positions where the sound is softer.
- Examples:
  - **saber** *to know* → [sa 'βeɾ]
  - **avión** *airplane* → [a 'βjon]

And now you can understand why you keep hearing two different pronunciations ☺

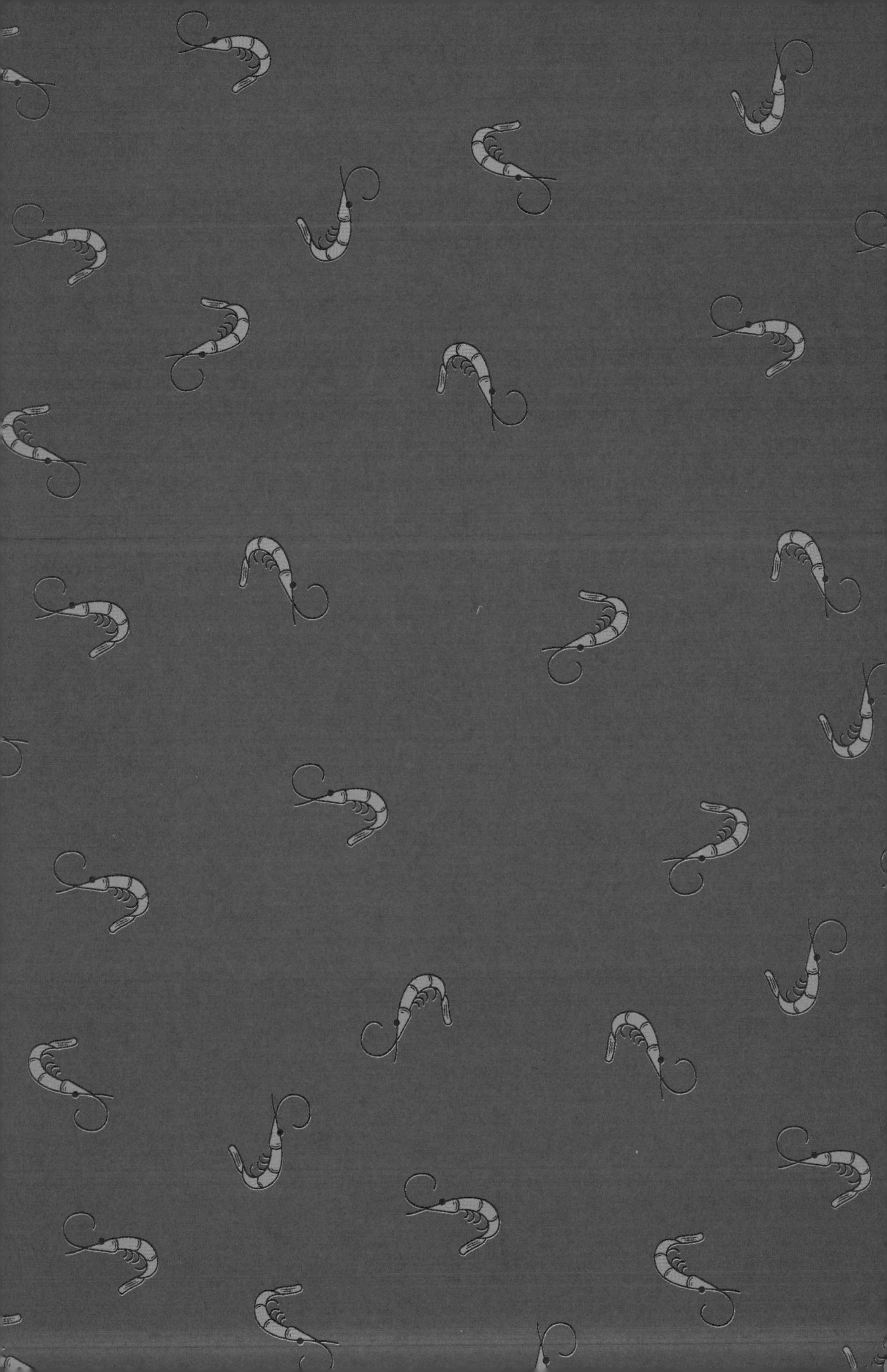

2

LA COCINA ESTÁ CERRADA

→ How to order in a café or a bar like a native

→ The rules of courtesy

→ Phrases that you need to know in a restaurant

→ The rules of paella

→ Understanding crazy Spanish schedules

→ Vocabulary basics: restaurants edition

HOW TO ORDER IN A CAFÉ OR A BAR LIKE A NATIVE

Don't say this if you don't want to sound like a robot! This is a literal translation from English and it doesn't work in SPANISH.

In Spain, people are way more informal than in Anglo-Saxon cultures. The way we express politeness is by adding **-ito**, **-illo** or **-ico** **(depending on the region)** to words, smiling and being friendly and affectionate.

¡ME PONES UN CAFECITO, POR FAVOR? (AND SMILE)

- ✔ un cafec**ito**/cafel**ito**
- ✔ una tap**ita**
- ✔ un vas**ito** de agua
- ✔ una cervec**ita** / una cañ**ita**

*Disculpe, **UNA** otra **CERVEZA**, por favor.

COMMON MISTAKE: in English you say "another."
But in Spanish, we don't say ***un otro*** or ***una otra***.
We simply say: **otro** or **otra**.

Another way to express politeness is by adding **cuando puedas** ("when you can") to any command:

OTRA CAÑA, CUANDO PUEDAS.

OK, now you are Spanish.

THE RULES OF COURTESY

In Spain, we don't overuse **gracias** and **por favor**. In Anglo-Saxon cultures, it is much more common to use those words to express politeness. But remember, Spanish people are informal. If you overuse those words, the conversation can feel awkward and unnatural.

Now you know this, how do you get the waitress' attention?

Spanish people, and especially women in their 30s or 40s, don't like being called **señor** or **señora** because it makes them feel old. You can use **señor** or **señora** with older people (remember Spanish people are always young lol) or in very elitist situations, like expensive restaurants or exclusive shops.

If you want to get someone's attention, it's better to say: **PERDONA** or **DISCULPA**. And that's it! ☺ **BUT** if you want to add more distance or respect, then use **usted**: **PERDONE** or **DISCULPE**.

Just be aware that in cities like **Barcelona** and **Madrid**, the use of **usted** is not as common as in villages and small cities.

Something else that might surprise you is that in Spain everybody is gorgeous. And if you don't believe me, just look at this:

CULTURAL TIP

Spanish people show politeness by being warm and friendly, often treating you with the care and affection you might expect from your mother or grandmother.

- ✔ guapo/a
- ✔ guapísimo/a
- ✔ cariño (for male and female)
- ✔ hermoso/a
- ✔ rey/reina

- ✔ precioso/a
- ✔ majo/a
- ✔ hijo/a
- ✔ corazón
- ✔ and in the south, **mi alma**

PHRASES THAT YOU NEED TO KNOW IN A RESTAURANT

How to book a table: 

Llamo para reservar una mesa para el sábado por la noche.
I am calling to reserve a table for Saturday night.

Me gustaría reservar una mesa para dos a las 9.
I'd like to reserve a table for two at 9.

Arriving at a restaurant: 

Tengo una reserva a nombre de...
I have a reservation under the name...

¿Tenéis mesa para dos?
Do you have a table for two?

¿Para cuántas personas? ¿Cuántos sois?
For how many people?

Somos cuatro. *There are four of us.*

¿Puedo sentarme aquí? *Can I sit here?*

¿Puedo ver la carta, por favor? *Can I see the menu, please?*
Don't say ***Puedo tener el menú.**

¿Tenéis una carta en inglés? *Do you have a menu in English?*

Ordering food: 

¿Qué me recomiendas?
What do you recommend?

¿Qué lleva este plato?
What's in this dish?

Voy a pedir...
I'll order... / I'll have...

¿Tenéis opciones vegetarianas/veganas?
Do you have vegetarian / vegan options?

¿Este plato lleva gluten / frutos secos / lácteos?
Does this dish contain gluten / nuts / dairy?

¿Me podrías traer una copa de vino tinto/blanco?
Could you bring me a glass of red / white wine?

¿Las croquetas, de qué son?
What's in the croquettes?

¿El filete, cómo lo quieres?
How do you want you steak?

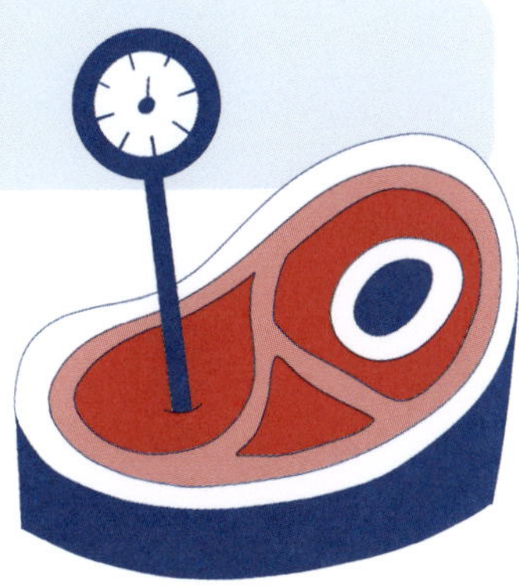

crudo *raw*
poco hecho *rare*
al punto *medium*
muy hecho *well done*

¿Podrías traer más pan, por favor?
Could you bring more bread, please?

¿Podrías traer más servilletas?
Could you bring more napkins?

El bistec está crudo. ¿Me lo podrías hacer un poco más?
*My steak is not fully cooked. Would you mind
cooking it a bit more?*

¿Falta mucho para que nos traigan la comida?
Will it take much longer for our food to arrive?

¿Me traerías un vaso de agua, por favor?
I'd like a glass of water, please.

Está frío, ¿me lo puede calentar?
It's cold. Could you warm it up for me?

¿Me podriáis traer un vasito de agua del grifo?
*Could you bring me a glass of tap water?
(I don't recommend this in Barcelona,
since the tap water tastes horrible.)*

Common mistake:
Don't say buen apetito. We say:

✔ **Que aproveche.**
✔ **Buen provecho.**

When the food is good: 

- **Está delicioso.** *It's delicious.*
- **Está riquísimo.** *It's incredibly tasty.*
- **Está buenísimo.** *It's really good.*
- **Está bestial.** *It's amazing.*
- **Está brutal.** *It's awesome.*
- **Está para chuparse los dedos.** *It's finger-licking good.*
- **Está de muerte.** *It's to die for.*
- **Está de rechupete.** *It's mouth-watering.*

When the food is not very good:

- **Está malísimo.** *It's awful.*
- **No se puede comer.** *It's inedible.*
- **Está crudo.** *It's undercooked.*
- **Está pasado.** *It's overcooked.*
- **Sabe mal.** *It tastes bad.*
- **Está duro.** *It's tough.*
- **Está quemado.** *It's burned.*
- **Está soso.** *It's bland.*
- **Le falta sal.** *It needs salt.*
- **Está picante.** *It's spicy.*
- **Está salado.** *It's salty.*

Paying the bill:

***Hola, me gustaría pagar, por favor.** Don't say this. Say:
La cuenta, cuando puedas.
The bill, when you get a chance.

¿Qué te debo? (informal)
What do I owe you?

¿Cuánto es todo?
How much is everything?

¿Me cobras, por favor?
Can you charge me, please?

Pagamos a medias.
Dividimos la cuenta.
We're splitting the bill.

¿Tienes cambio de 50?
Do you have change for a 50?

Pago yo.
I'll pay.

Te invito yo.
I'll treat you.

Cada uno paga lo suyo.
Everyone pays for their own meal/drink.

To take away:

CULTURAL TIP

¡PROPINA?

IN SPAIN, WE DON'T USUALLY LEAVE A "TIP."

In Spain, leaving a tip (**dejar propina**) is not a common practice as it is in many other countries. While it's appreciated, especially in tourist areas, it's not expected and often seen as unnecessary. The service charge is typically included in the bill and waitstaff are generally compensated fairly for their work. Spaniards may occasionally round up the bill or leave small change as a gesture of appreciation, but it's not a formal obligation.

THE RULES OF PAELLA

Since we are talking about food and restaurants, I think it's the right time to talk about the most famous Spanish dish of all time: paella. And let me tell you some important rules that you must bear in mind if you don't want to come off as a tourist:

1. Paella is for sharing (unless it's on the daily special menu), and not for dinner.

2. Never pair it with sangría, as this combo is only for tourists. Choose wine.

3. Eat paella only in the Valencian Community or along the Mediterranean coast.

4. Avoid ordering it in northern Spain (like Galicia or the Basque Country).

5. Don't add chorizo, ham or coriander. This is a crime.

6. Authentic paella valenciana includes rabbit, chicken, sometimes even snails and green beans.

7. Don't call just any rice dish "paella." This is a serious offense in Valencia.

8. Remember all these rules and you will be safe! ☺

UNDERSTANDING CRAZY SPANISH SCHEDULES

In Spain, the concept of time often feels quite different from what many are accustomed to, leading to the saying **"The kitchen is closed."** This phrase reflects the common practice of shutting down restaurants during the **siesta**, a traditional afternoon break.

Many restaurants open for lunch time (from 12 or 1 PM to 4 or 5 PM) and they close the kitchen after lunch and they open it again for dinner (around 8 PM). So sometimes they will tell you **la cocina está cerrada** if you go at 6 PM, and you can only have a drink.

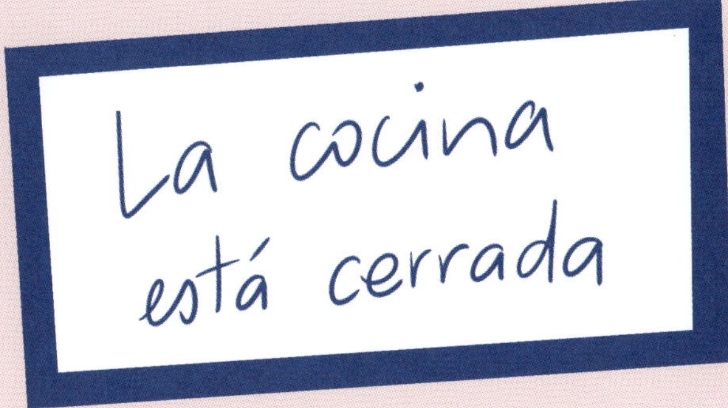

VOCABULARY BASICS: RESTAURANTS EDITION

		LO SABÍA	NO LO SABÍA
appetizer	aperitivo		
first course	primer plato		
main course	segundo plato		
dessert	postre		
menu	carta		
daily special menu	menú del día		
plate	plato		
glass	vaso		
wine glass	copa		
napkin	servilleta		
knife	cuchillo		
spoon	cuchara		
teaspoon	cucharilla		
side dish	acompañamiento		
tip	propina		
to go	para llevar		
to reserve	reservar		
deep plate	plato hondo		
flat plate	plato llano		
cup	taza		
tablecloth	mantel		
to season	aliñar		

3

¿QUIERES BOLSA?

- → How to describe food gone bad
- → How to shop in Spanish markets
- → Useful sentences in a small shop / market
- → Like a native: informal expressions with food

HOW TO DESCRIBE FOOD GONE BAD

Imagine that you open the fridge and this is the situation:

El yogurt está **caducado**: *expired*
El pan está **duro**: *stale*
El queso está **mohoso**: *moldy*
La leche está **agria**: *spoiled*
La fruta está **podrida**: *rotten*

YOU CAN SIMPLY SAY:
TODA LA COMIDA ESTÁ MALA.

OK, I think it's time to go shopping:

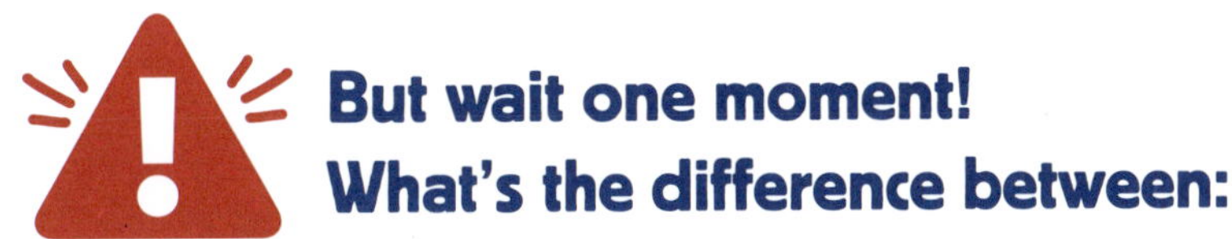

This means doing
the shopping
(usually for groceries).

This means going
shopping (generally
for clothes, shoes, etc.).

Perfecto, ¡pues vamos a hacer la compra!

HOW TO SHOP IN SPANISH MARKETS

¡DÓNDE PODEMOS HACER LA COMPRA?

En el supermercado, por supuesto.

En el mercado:

A place where fresh goods like fruits, vegetables and meat are sold. It can be indoors or outdoors.

En el mercadillo:

A small, temporary outdoor market where second-hand items, crafts and cheap goods are sold.

En una tienda de barrio de toda la vida:

A **tienda de barrio** is a small, family-run store located in a residential area. These stores have been around for generations and are convenient places for locals to buy daily essentials.

Why are they called **de toda la vida**? The phrase **de toda la vida** translates to **"life-long"** or **"long-standing,"** meaning that these stores have been part of the neighborhood for as long as people can remember. They evoke nostalgia and are associated with tradition and trust.

CAN YOU WRITE THE NAME OF THESE SPANISH SHOPS FOLLOWING THE SAME PATTERN?

fruta FRUT**ERÍA**

zapatos ZAPAT**ERÍA**

joyas ___________

verduras ___________

pescado ___________

carne ___________

helados ___________

libros ___________

flores ___________

juguetes ___________

perfumes ___________

pan ___________

pasteles ___________

pelo ___________

papel ___________

té ___________

Soluciones: zapatería, joyería, verdulería, pescadería, carnicería, heladería, librería, floristería, juguetería, perfumería, panadería, pastelería, peluquería, papelería, tetería

USEFUL SENTENCES IN A SMALL SHOP / MARKET

I know that shopping in a traditional store can be intimidating when you're a foreigner and don't speak the language well, but don't worry. Here are some useful phrases so you can do it with confidence:

¿Quién es el último?

Who is the last person in line?

Perdona, te has colado.

Excuse me, you've cut in line.

Estaba yo primero.

I was here first.

¿A cuánto están las manzanas?

How much are the apples?

¿Qué precio tiene el kilo de tomates?

What's the price per kilo of tomatoes?

¿Está fresco?

Is this fresh?

¿Esto está de oferta?

Is this on sale?

¿Los aguacates están maduros?

Are the avocados ripe?

¿Cuánto es todo?

How much is everything?

¿Puedo pagar con tarjeta / en efectivo?

Can I pay by card / in cash?

¿Me puede dar una bolsa, por favor?

Can you give me a bag, please?

En la carnicería:

Quería un kilo de cordero. *I'd like a kilo of mutton.*

Quiero medio kilo de carne picada.
I'd like half a kilo of ground meat.

¿Puedes cortarlo en filetes/rodajas/trozos?
Can you cut it into slices/rings/pieces?

Sin hueso, por favor. *Without bones, please.*

¿Me lo puedes preparar para guisar?
Can you prepare it for stewing?

¿Me pones 250 gramos de jamón serrano?
Can you give me 250 grams of serrano ham?

En la pescadería:

Quiero medio kilo de lubina.
I'd like half kilo of sea bass.

¿Me lo puedes limpiar? *Can you clean it for me?*

Quiero el pescado entero / en filetes.
I want the fish whole / in fillets.

¿Puedes quitarle las espinas? *Can you remove the bones?*

¿Puedes prepararlo para la plancha / el horno?
Can you prepare it for the grill / the oven?

Examples of interesting products that you will find in a Spanish supermarket:

- Ham-flavored potato chips.
- A wide variety of olives that you can pick yourself.
- Olive oil in 5-liter jugs.
- Cured meats: ham, chorizo, salchichón, fuet.
- Ham legs.
- Cheese. Lots of cheese.
- Wine. Lots of wine.
- Gazpacho in cartons.
- Spanish potato omelet (**tortilla de patata de toda la vida**).
- Legumes in canned jars.
- Individual cans of Coca-Cola or beer.
- Fresh orange juice you can squeeze yourself.
- Milk and eggs out of the fridge.

WHICH ONE SURPRISES YOU THE MOST?

COMMON MISTAKES:

Learning a language isn't just about memorizing vocabulary and grammar rules. It's about diving into a new culture, customs, and —of course— avoiding those little mix-ups that can lead to funny or even awkward moments.

Did you know that, in Spain, asking for a **bolso** instead of a **bolsa** can make a big difference? If you walk into a store and say "I'd like to buy a black **bolsa** made of leather" the shop assistant might give you a confused look. That's because a **bolsa** is usually a plastic or fabric bag, while a **bolso** is a stylish handbag.

And what about **tíquet** vs. **billete**? In English, *ticket* usually refers to a train ticket or a movie ticket, but in Spain, a **tíquet** is just a receipt that you are given after any purchase. If you need to travel by train, make sure to ask for a **billete** or you might end up stuck at the station!

Spanish is full of tricky words that often confuse English speakers, but once you master them, you'll feel like a true Spanish pro.

Be careful with these confusing words:

UN BOLSO

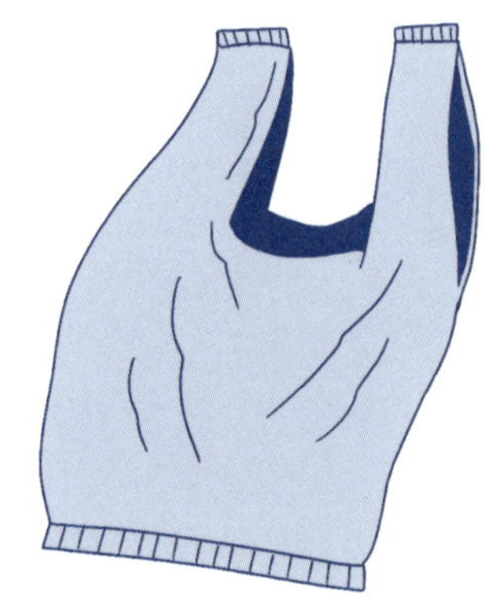

UNA BOLSA

UNA CESTA

UN BILLETE

UN TÍQUET

UNA ENTRADA

UNA TARJETA

UNA CARTA

UN PEZ (ALIVE)

UN PESCADO (DEAD)

HOW ADVANCED IS YOUR VOCABULARY?

a packet of rice	un _____________ de arroz
a can of beer	una _____________ de cerveza
a bag of potatoes	una _____________ de patatas
a bunch of grapes	un _____________ de uvas
a clove of garlic	un _____________ de ajo
a dozen eggs	una _____________ de huevos
a jar of olives	un _____________ de aceitunas
a handful of walnuts	un _____________ de nueces
a bottle of milk	una _____________ de leche
a carton of wine	un _____________ de vino
a box of cookies	una _____________ de galletas
a fillet of hake	un _____________ de merluza
a slice of cheese	una _____________ de queso
a ring of pineapple	una _____________ de piña
a slice of bread	una _____________ de pan
a piece of cake	un _____________ de pastel

LIKE A NATIVE: INFORMAL EXPRESSIONS WITH FOOD

Spanish has many informal expressions using the word "milk" and other foods:

ser la leche *to be unbelievable* (good and bad)
estar de mala leche *to be in a bad mood*
tener mala leche *to have a bad temper*
ir a toda leche *to be very fast*
darse una leche *to fall*
cagarse en la leche (OK, this is a swear word)
importar un pepino *to not care*
ser pan comido *easy peasy / a piece of cake*
ir a freír espárragos *go take a hike*
ser la pera *you're the best*

And of course eggs are no exception:

un huevo means *"a lot"*
Hay un huevo de gente. *There are a lot of people.*

But also:

Me importa un huevo. *I don't care at all.*

Yes, Spanish people are weird.

4

¿NOS CONOCEMOS?

HOW TO FLIRT (OR NOT) IN SPANISH

Imagine you walk into a Spanish bar and fall in love at first sight (**tienes un flechazo**) with a handsome guy or beautiful girl.

How do you flirt? Cómo **LIGAR** como un español:

COMPLIMENT THE PERSON:
HACER UN CUMPLIDO:

Pareces mucho más joven. *You look a lot younger.*

¿Quién lo diría? *Who would have thought?*

Pensaba que tenías muchos menos. *I thought you were much younger.*

Te conservas genial. *You look great for your age.*

Estás estupendo/a. *You look amazing.*

Ya me gustaría a mí llegar así. *I'd love to look like that at your age.*

¿Dónde hay que firmar para llegar así?
Where do I sign to look like that?

GRAMMAR TIP

The suffix -azo will help you compliment anyone in Spanish:

ojos	**eyes**	oj**azos**	very beautiful eyes
pelo	**hair**	pel**azo**	very beautiful hair
cuerpo	**body**	cuerp**azo**	very beautiful body
culo	**butt**	cul**azo**	very nice butt
moreno	**tanned**	moren**azo**	hunk

¡Qué oj**azos** tienes!

¡Vaya pel**azo**!

¡Menudo cuerp**azo**!

The suffix **-azo** is a versatile tool in Spanish, often used to emphasize the size, importance or intensity of something. It can make words sound bigger, stronger or more extreme.

¡Vaya cochAZO tienes!

Now imagine the opposite situation. Someone annoying is trying to flirt with you.

How to reject him or her (cómo RECHAZAR a alguien):

polite: educado

Sorry, I'm waiting for my friend and I don't feel like it. Thanks.

I really appreciate it, but I'm already in a relationship.

rude: maleducado

Don't be annoying!

Don't bother me!

Leave me alone!

Go to hell!

MEETING NEW PEOPLE

DO YOU KNOW WHAT TO DO WHEN YOU ARE INTRODUCED TO SOMEONE?

Mira, te presento a mi novio.
Hola, encantado (if you are male) **encantada** (if you are female)
or **Mucho gusto** (Pleasure to meet you).

CULTURAL TIP

In Spain, we always give two kisses when we are introduced to someone, regardless of age or gender, although it's more common between women or between men and women (two men shake hands). This can even happen in formal work situations, even though it is more common to shake hands in that context. Sometimes, if you don't give two kisses, the situation can become awkward and the person may feel that you are rude. It's also important to notice that we don't hug. Hugging is very intimate and we only do it with friends and family.

Asking someone their age is very common when you first meet: **¿Cuántos años tienes?** And every time you ask someone this question, they will answer: **¿Cuántos me echas?** (How old do you think I am?)

Be careful, because it's a tricky question. To be safe, you should always say 5 years younger than what you think. And if you put your foot in it, just throw in a compliment like I showed you!

HOW TO SUGGEST A PLAN

Now that you already have Spanish friends, let's learn how to **suggest a plan**:

¿Quedamos este viernes? *Shall we meet this Friday?*

¿Te apetece ir a cenar esta noche?
Do you feel like going out for dinner tonight?

¿Salimos hoy? *Should we go out tonight?*

¿Haces algo esta noche? *Are you doing anything tonight?*

¿Te vienes a mi casa y luego salimos por ahí?
Wanna come to my place and then go out?

¿Tomamos algo hoy? *Shall we grab a drink today?*

¿Nos vemos este sábado? *See you on Saturday?*

¿Qué te parece si vamos al cine? *How about going to the movies?*

COMMON MISTAKE:
If you want to say: "Is it OK for you?", don't say:
*__¿Está bien para ti?__ (This a literal translation from English and it sounds weird.)
We say:
✔ **¿Te va bien? ¿Te viene bien?**
✔ **¿Te parece bien?**
✔ **¿Qué tal te va?**
✔ **¿Te apuntas?** *Are you in?*
✔ **¿Te vienes?** *Are you coming?*

Now you can **agree to the plan by** saying:

Me apunto. *I'm in.*
Me va genial. *It's perfect for me.*
Me parece estupendo. *Sounds good.*
Nos vemos allí. *See you there.*
Te veo ahí.
Quedamos ahí. *Let's meet there.*
A las diez en plaza Cataluña.

And your Spanish friend can say:

This means that you want to go out in a chill or low-key way. Spanish people always say this, but the opposite always ends up happening and you end up getting "tangled up" (**siempre nos liamos**), meaning drinking too much and going to bed super late.

Spanish punctuality: to be late as a way of life

In Spain, punctuality isn't overly strict. For informal gatherings, it's acceptable to arrive 10 to 20 minutes late. However, when it comes to work, it's important to be punctual.

So how do you say "I'm late" when you need it?

But sometimes we are still in the shower and we say:

HOW TO REJECT A PLAN

We Spaniards don't say no directly. In fact, we often drag it out.

Si eso ya te digo algo. *I'll let you know.*
Lo vamos viendo. *We'll see.*
Vamos hablando. *We'll talk.*
Te doy un toque. *I'll call you.*

MAÑANA te digo algo.
(Most of the time the word **mañana** means **NEVER**.)

GRAMMAR TIP

Whenever you reject a plan, give an explanation; otherwise you'll seem rude, and you're not rude. So how to do it? It's easy just follow this rule:

ES QUE + **ANY EXCUSE**

For example: **No puedo, es que mi perro tiene diarrea.**

MORE THAN FRIENDS: RELATIONSHIPS IN SPAIN

TE QUIERO VS TE AMO

There are cultural differences between Latin America and Spain. **Te quiero** is the usual way to say "I love you" in Spain, but in Latin America it's used with friends. **Te amo** is used with your lover to express a deeper love. In Spain, **te amo** sounds corny or cheesy and we don't use it that much.

CHEESY NICKNAMES: APODOS CURSIS:

cuqui
gordi
churri
guapi
princesa/príncipe
rey/reina
mi amor
bebé
mi vida
mi alma
corazón
cari
cielo
cosita
amorcito
bizcochito

USEFUL SENTENCES THAT YOU WILL NEED WHEN YOU HAVE AN ARGUMENT WITH YOUR PARTNER:

Here you are sad and disappointed.

Here you are angry and want to fight.

No me hablas.
No te preocupas por mí.
No me escuchas
No me miras.
No me esperas
No me tocas.

¡No me hables!
¡No te preocupes por mí!
¡No me escuches!
¡No me mires!
¡No me esperes!
¡No me toques!

This is a statement

This is a command

Notice that the sentences in the left column are in the **presente simple** and the ones in the right column are in the **imperativo** and the **negativo**, which takes the same conjugation as the **presente de subjuntivo**. In some verbs only one letter can make the difference!

CAN YOU TRANSLATE THESE WORDS?

conocerse ______________

tener un flechazo ______________

enamorarse ______________

salir juntos ______________

comprometerse ______________

casarse ______________

poner los cuernos ______________

tener celos ______________

discutir ______________

pelear ______________

romper con alguien ______________

separarse ______________

divorciarse ______________

pareja ______________

cita ______________

echar de menos ______________

novio ______________

desamor ______________

Soluciones: to meet; to have a crush; to fall in love; to date; to get engaged; to get married; to cheat (on someone); to be jealous; to argue; to fight; to break up (with someone); to separate; to get divorced; partner/couple; date; to miss (someone); boyfriend; heartbreak

PRONUNCIATION BASICS: INFORMAL

In Spain and other Spanish-speaking countries, we usually don't pronounce the "d" in words ending in **-ado**:

CANSADO ⟶ **CANSAO**   **PESADO** ⟶ **PESAO**

We also don't pronounce certain letters in certain words. Here you have some informal pronunciation tips to understand native speakers:

para: **pa'**
todo: **to'**
para acá: **pa'cá**
para allá: **pa'llá**
hasta luego: **ta luego** or **ta logo**
entonces: **tonces**

5

SOY BUENO Y ESTOY BUENO

⟶ Embarrassing mistakes you want to avoid

⟶ How to use the verbs **ser** and **estar**

⟶ Using **ser** and **estar** with adjectives

⟶ Talking about your mood and personality

EMBARRASING MISTAKES YOU WANT TO AVOID

Apparently this guy thinks he's hot.

I'm sure you have made these very embarrassing mistakes like the man before. Let's correct them if you don't want to feel embarrassed:

COMMON MISTAKES:

	It doesn't mean	It means
Estoy bueno/a.	I'm OK.	I'm hot.
Estoy embarazado/a.	I'm embarrassed.	I'm pregnant.
Estoy caliente.	I'm hot.	I'm horny.
Estoy excitado/a.	I'm excited.	I'm horny.

If you want to say:	You have to say:
I'm OK.	✔ **Estoy bien.**
I'm embarrassed.	✔ **Me da vergüenza** or **Estoy avergonzado/a.** (less common)
I'm hot.	✔ **Tengo calor.**
I'm excited.	✔ **Me hace ilusión** or **Estoy ilusionado/a.** (less common)

What are they talking about? This is so tricky... like a puzzle.

HOW TO USE THE VERBS
SER AND ESTAR

Take a look at this:

***ES BIEN.**

ESTÁ BIEN.
He/She feels OK.

ES BUENO.

It is healthy, good.

ESTÁ BUENO.

It is tasty.

ESTÁ BIEN.

It is OK, correct, adequate.

SER
Es malo.
He is a bad person or not
a good professional.

ESTAR
Está malo/a.
He is sick.

***ES MAL.**

ESTÁ MAL.
He feels bad. / He is not OK.

ES MALO.
It is bad, not healthy.

ESTÁ MALO/A.
It is not tasty or
in bad condition.

***ES MAL.**

ESTÁ MAL.
It is incorrect, not OK
inadequate.

Oh yes, I get it:

The reality is that this "solution" doesn't work and most of the time it is the reason why you keep making mistakes with ser and estar.

Instead of permanent and temporary, think about the concepts of characteristics (**ser**) and circumstances (**estar**). It doesn't matter whether these characteristics and circumstances are going to last forever or not.

El cielo es azul.

Is the sky going to be blue forever?
Well, if you live in London, I don't think so.

But why didn't anybody ever tell me this before?

Well, that is still an unsolved mystery, but luckily, you've come across this book and now you are one of the fortunate ones who know all the secrets about **ser** and **estar**.

USING SER AND ESTAR WITH ADJECTIVES

Imagine you're watching a dramatic Spanish **telenovela**. The heroine, María, sighs dramatically and says:

Juan is so handsome...

But he looks always so ugly...

Wait —what? How can Juan be handsome and ugly at the same time? Is he cursed? A shapeshifter? Or is this just another Spanish grammar mystery waiting to be solved?

Well, dear reader, welcome to one of the trickiest (but most fun!) aspects of Spanish: the difference between **ser** and **estar** when used with adjectives.

You see, Spanish doesn't just have one verb for "to be" —it has two. And choosing between them can change the entire meaning of a sentence.

That's why with most adjectives you can use both **ser** and **estar**, depending on whether you're talking about **characteristics** or **circumstances**:

◆ **SER** + **adjective** → Describes an essential characteristic, something that defines a person or thing. (Juan is handsome.)

◆ **ESTAR** + **adjective** → Describes a circumstance. (Today, Juan *looks* ugly —maybe he didn't sleep well, or he got a terrible haircut.)

See? No magic, just grammar! But don't worry. By the end of this chapter, you'll know exactly when to use **ser** and when to use **estar**, and you won't need a telenovela to figure it out.

Here's another example:

Is she going to be beautiful forever?
We don't know and it's irrelevant.

Is she going to look beautiful forever?
We don't know and it's irrelevant.

He is young.

She looks or feels young
(even if she is old).

It is new.

It looks new, it's in good
condition (even if it is old).

He is old.

He looks or feels old
(even if he is young).

ES VIEJO.   ESTÁ VIEJO.

It is old.   It looks old, it's not in good condition (even if it is new).

But sometimes, the adjective will change the meaning according to this:

ES		ESTÁ
prideful	**orgulloso**	*feeling proud*
smart	**listo**	*ready*
green	**verde**	*inexperienced or not ripe*
mature	**maduro**	*ripe*
rich	**rico**	*tasty*
open-minded	**abierto**	*open*
closed-minded	**cerrado**	*closed*
attentive	**atento**	*paying attention*
motivated by self-interest	**interesado**	*interested*

TALKING ABOUT YOUR MOOD AND PERSONALITY

With feelings and emotions, you will always use the verb **estar**, since emotions are circumstantial:

ESTOY TRISTE:
Estoy de bajón.
Estoy desanimado/a.
Estoy hundido/a.
I'm sad.

ESTOY CANSADO/A:
Estoy agotado/a.
Estoy que me caigo.
Estoy para el arrastre.
I'm tired.

ESTOY ENFADADO/A:
Estoy cabreado/a.
Estoy de mal humor.
Estoy quemado/a.
I'm angry.

ESTOY PREOCUPADO/A:
Estoy rayado/a.
Estoy inquieto/a.
Estoy intranquilo/a.
I'm worried.

ESTOY CONTENTO/A:
Estoy feliz.
Estoy de buen humor.
Estoy eufórico/a.
I'm happy.

ESTOY CONFUNDIDO/A:
Estoy hecho un lío.
Estoy perdido/a.
Estoy descolocado/a.
I'm confused.

WE USE THE VERB SER TO DESCRIBE CHARACTERISTICS. HERE ARE SOME SPANISH PERSONALITIES.

Which kind of person are you? Don't lie 😉

- ☐ **un/una borde**
  rude

- ☐ **un/una cotilla**
  a gossip

- ☐ **un/una quejica**
  a complainer

- ☐ **un/una crack**
  an expert/ace

- ☐ **un/una cabezota**
  a stubborn person

- ☐ **un vago / una vaga**
  a lazy person

- ☐ **un/una plasta**
  a pain-in-the-ass

- ☐ **un/una sabelotodo**
  a know-it-all

- ☐ **un soso / una sosa**
  a dull person

- ☐ **una pesado / una pesada**
  an annoying/boring person

- ☐ **un mandón / una mandona**
  a bossy person

- ☐ **un/una tiquismiquis**
  a fussy person

6

DE COMPRAS

- → Get dressed in Spanish
- → Let's go shopping
- → How to buy shoes
- → After shopping: estrenar... o devolver

GET DRESSED IN SPANISH

Are you one of those people like me who open the closet and say:
"I have nothing to wear"?

First, let me tell you that we use some Spanish words in their singular
form, even if the plural form does exist. For example:

la ropa	las ropas
la gente	las gentes
el pelo	los pelos
el marisco	los mariscos

un **pantalón** *pants* ☐

unos **vaqueros** *jeans* ☐

unos **pantalones cortos** *shorts* ☐

una **falda** *skirt* ☐

un **vestido** *dress* ☐

un **abrigo** *coat* ☐

una **chaqueta** *jacket* ☐

una **chaqueta de cuero** *leather jacket* ☐

un **impermeable** *raincoat* ☐

un **suéter** / un **jersey** *sweater* ☐

una **sudadera** *hoodie* ☐

un **chaleco** *vest* ☐

una **bufanda** *scarf* ☐

unos **guantes** *gloves* ☐

un **traje** *suit* ☐

una **corbata** *tie* ☐

un **pijama** *pajamas* ☐

un **bañador** *swimsuit* ☐

ropa interior *underwear* ☐

un **sujetador** *bra* ☐

unas **bragas** *panties* ☐

unos **calzoncillos** *men's underwear* ☐

unas **medias** *stockings* ☐

unos **calcetines** *socks* ☐

A LITTLE TRICK SO YOU REMEMBER THIS VOCABULARY

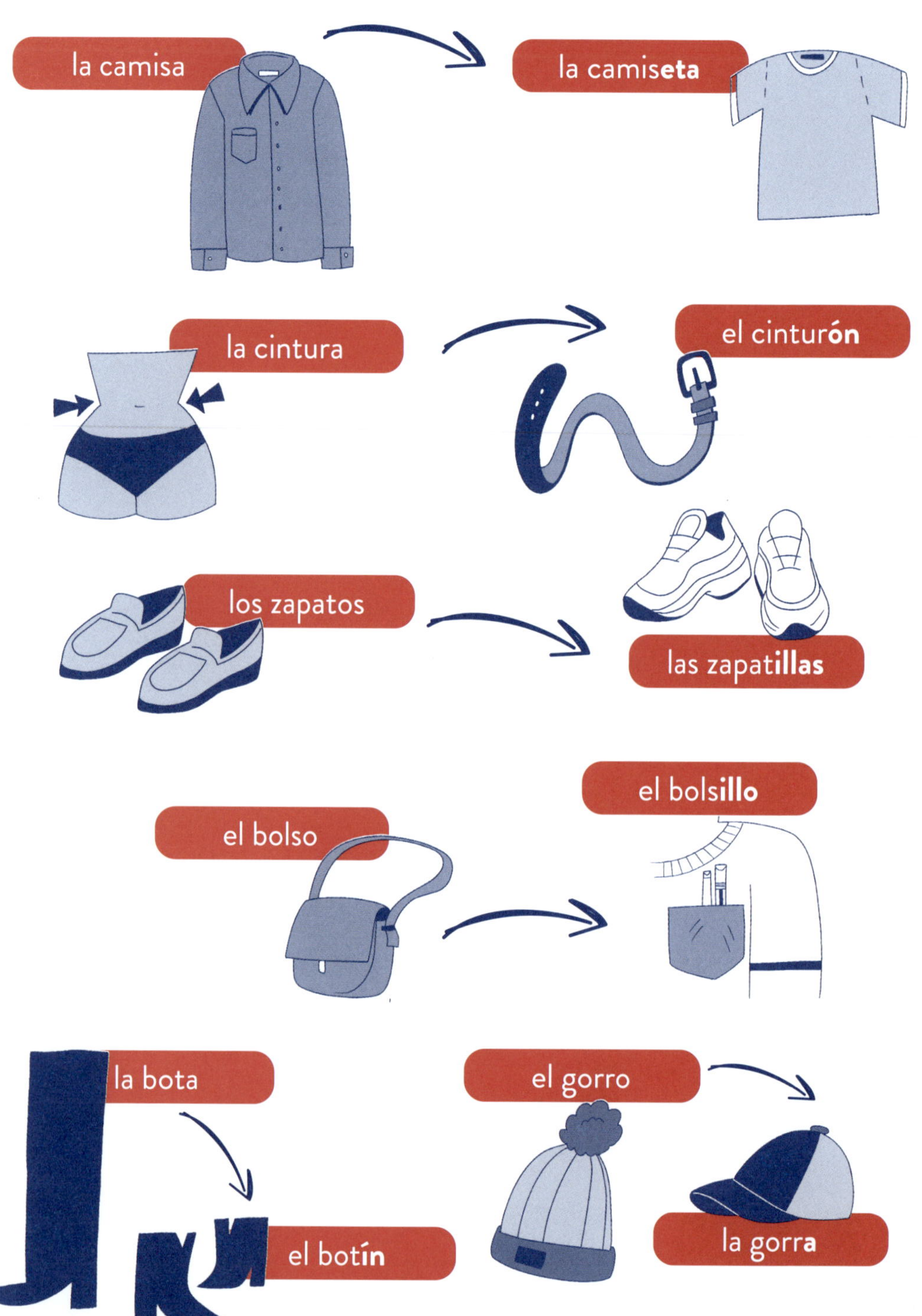

Mono means: monkey, overalls and cute.

LET'S GO SHOPPING

Shopping in Spain can be a fun experience, but it can also be a bit challenging if you're not confident with the language yet. How do you ask for a **barra de pan** at the bakery without just pointing? What do you say when the cashier asks if you need a **bolsa** (remember the past lessons)? And what if you need to return something?

Pero no te preocupes. In this chapter, you'll learn key phrases and multiple tips to help you feel confident when doing your shopping.

WHEN ENTERING THE SHOP:

Every time you enter a shop, you'll be asked:

¿Te puedo ayudar en algo? or
¿En qué te puedo ayudar? *Can I help you?*

Option 1: No, gracias, solo estoy mirando. *I'm just browsing.*

Option 2: **Sí, estoy buscando una camisa...**

| que **es** de lunares. | que **sea** de lunares. |

When I'm talking about a specific shirt that I know and I saw in the shop.

When I'm looking for something but don't know if they have it in the shop.

I USE THE INDICATIVO

I'm looking for a shirt with polka dots. → I know you have it here, but I can't find it.

I USE THE SUBJUNTIVO

I'm looking for a shirt with polka dots. → I don't know whether you have it here because I haven't seen it.

More useful sentences

¿Puedo probarme esta camisa/blusa?
Can I try on this shirt/blouse?

¿Dónde están los probadores?
Where are the fitting rooms?

¿Tienen esta prenda en otro color / otra talla?
Do you have this item in another color/size?

¿Lo tienes en una talla más grande/pequeña?
Do you have it in a bigger/smaller size?

In the fitting room: ¡Cómo me queda este vestido!

- **Estás guapísima.** *You're so beautiful.*
- **Te sienta genial.** *It fits you well.*
- **El color te favorece.** *That color suits you.*
- **Te ves muy elegante.** *You look very elegant.*
- **Te queda como un guante.** *It fits you like a glove.*

tu amiga ser de luz

tu amiga sincera

- **Te va grande. / Te queda pequeño.** *It's too big/small for you.*
- **No te favorece.** *It doesn't suit you.*
- **No te pega. / No es de tu estilo.** *It's not your style.*
- **Te ves mayor.** *It makes you look older.*
- **Te hace más bajita.** *It makes you look shorter.*

Talking about the price

¡QUÉ BARATO! *How cheap!*

Está de rebajas. *It's on sale.*
Es un chollo. *It's a bargain.*
Es una ganga. *It's a bargain.*
Está tirado de precio.
  It's very cheap.
Es una baratija.
  (negative sense)

¡QUÉ CARO! *How expensive!*

Es un robo. *It's highway robbery.*
Es un timo. *It's a scam.*
Vale un ojo de la cara.
Cuesta un riñón.
Está por las nubes.
Es carísimo.
→ *It's very expensive.*

In English it costs an arm and a leg, but in Spanish it costs an eye of the face or a kidney:

The moment of truth

If you like it:

Me gusta, me la/lo llevo.
I like it. I'll take it.

If you don't like it and just want to leave, give an excuse:

No estoy seguro/a. Me lo voy a pensar.
I'm not sure. Can I think about it?

Me doy una vuelta y vuelvo.
I'll go for a walk and come back.

¿A qué hora cerráis? Me paso luego.
What time do you close? I'll come back later.

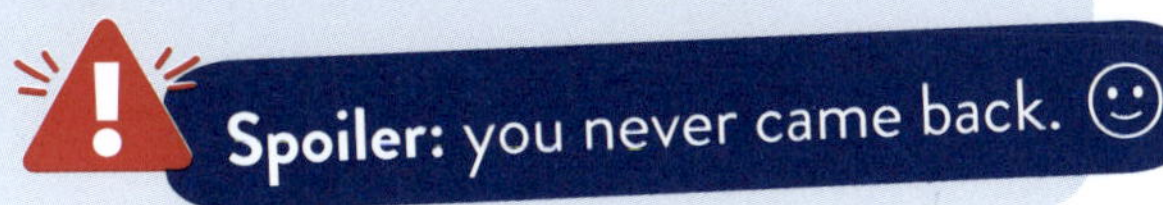

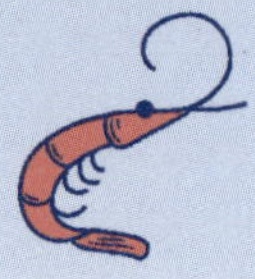

Examples of REGATEO IN A MERCADILLO

But wait: if you are in a **mercadillo** (a bazaar or an informal market) you can sometimes negotiate the price. In Spanish, to haggle is **REGATEAR**.

HOW TO BUY SHOES

NOW THAT YOU KNOW HOW TO SHOP IN STORES, WHAT ABOUT BUYING SOMETHING FOR DAILY USE, LIKE A PAIR OF NEW SHOES?

El calzado: footwear

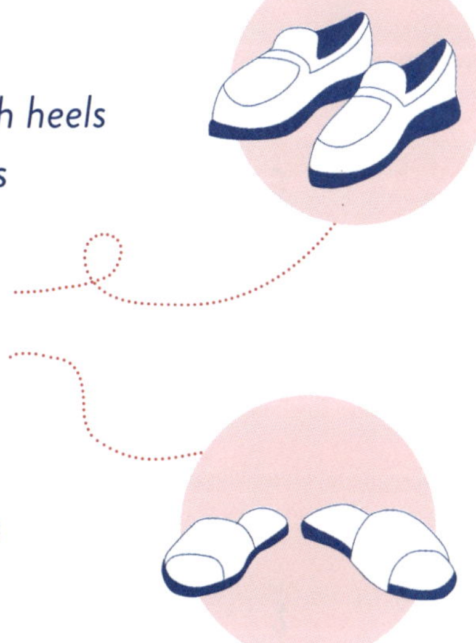

las zapatillas *sneakers*
los zapatos *shoes*
los zapatos de tacón *high heels*
las botas altas *high boots*
los botines *ankle boots*
los mocasines *loafers*
las chanclas *flip-flops*
las pantuflas *slippers*
las sandalias *sandals*
las alpargatas *espadrilles*
las bailarinas *ballet flats*
los zuecos *clogs*
las botas de agua *rain boots*

CULTURAL TIP

Depending on the region you live you will hear different ways to say "sneakers":

ZAPAS, BAMBAS, PLAYERAS, TENIS

EN LA ZAPATERÍA

I'm looking for comfortable shoes.

____

Do you have this model in size 38?

____

Can I try on these shoes?

____

They fit me well/poorly.

____

They're too tight/wide.

____

Are they made of leather?

____

Can I return them if they don't fit me?

____

Soluciones: Estoy buscando unos zapatos cómodos. / ¿Tienen este modelo en talla/número 38? / ¿Tienes un 38 de este modelo? / ¿Puedo probarme estos zapatos? / Me quedan bien/mal. / Me van bien/mal. / Son demasiado ajustados/anchos. / ¿Son de cuero? / ¿Puedo devolverlos si no me van bien?

AFTER SHOPPING: ESTRENAR... O DEVOLVER

Now that you've been shopping, you have two options with your new purchases. If you love them, it's time to wear them for the first time (yaaay!). And if you're not convinced... you can always return them! (booo)

Yes, I keep it! Time to estrenar

Now that you have bought your dress, you can **estrenar el vestido**. **Estrenar** means to use something for the first time. It's a versatile verb that can refer to clothing, movies, possessions or even actions.

Hoy estreno zapatos nuevos.
Today I'm wearing new shoes for the first time.

Estrenar is also commonly used in the entertainment industry to refer to the release or premiere of a movie, play or song.

La película se estrena mañana en los cines.
The movie premieres tomorrow in theaters.

Hmm I don't like it at all. Time to return it

Imagine that you try your new dress on at home, but you don't like it and want to return it:

Está descolorido.
It's faded.
La cremallera está rota.
The zipper is broken.
Está deshilachado.
It's frayed.
Está manchado.
It's stained
Está descosido.
It's unstiched.
Le faltan botones.
It's missing buttons.
Los bolsillos están agujereados.
The pockets have holes.

What's the problem

Vale, ¿tienes el tíquet?
Do you have the receipt?

Remember: the word tíquet in Spanish means "receipt."

¿Te hago un reembolso, o quieres cambiarlo por otra cosa?

Do you want me to give you a refund,
or would you like to exchange it for something else?

7

EN FAMILIA

FAMILY VOCABULARY

Family is one of the most important parts of life, if not the most, and talking about it is essential in any language.

Whether you're introducing your relatives, asking about someone's family, or describing relationships...

... here are some family related words that will help you for sure!

el padre *father*
la madre *mother*
el hermano *brother*
la hermana *sister*
el abuelo *grandfather*
la abuela *grandmother*
el hijo *son*
la hija *daughter*
el tío *uncle*
la tía *aunt*
el primo *cousin (male)*
la prima *cousin (female)*
el suegro *father-in-law*
la suegra *mother-in-law*

el yerno *son-in-law*
la nuera *daughter-in-law*
el cuñado *brother-in-law*
la cuñada *sister-in-law*
el sobrino *nephew*
la sobrina *niece*
el marido *husband*
la mujer *wife*
los padres *parents*
los hijos *children/kids*
el padrino *godfather*
la madrina *godmother*
el ahijado *godson*
la ahijada *goddaughter*

Estos son mis **padres.**

These are my parents.

Estos son mis **parientes.**

These are my relatives.
(We can also say **familiares.***)*

TENGO DOS PADRES Y MUCHOS PARIENTES.
I have two parents and a lot of relatives.

PARECER VS PARECERSE

In families, it's common to look like one another. How can you say this in Spanish?

PARECER	PARECERSE A
to seem / to look like: when we compare someone in general	when we compare someone with a specific person
Mi abuela **parece** una actriz. (the profession)	Mi abuela **se parece** a Sara Montiel. (a specific person)

In Spanish we don't say "like two peas in a pod." We say "like two drops of water": **Somos como dos gotas de agua.**

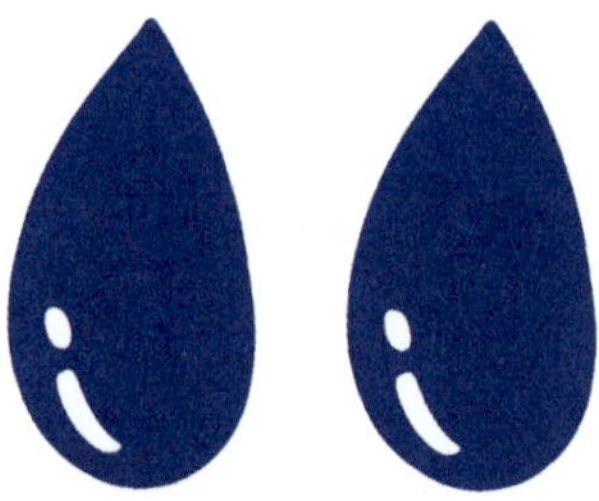

Y tú, ¡a quién te pareces?

CULTURAL TIP

In Spain, we use the word **tío** when talking about our family member (our mother's or father's brother). But we also use it to refer to friends or even strangers. In fact, **tío** is probably one of the most commonly used words in Spanish, and you've surely heard it hundreds of times in thousands of different contexts!

DISCOVERING THE YAYAS

In many Spanish regions, we call our grandmother **yaya**. Here are some things you can find in every Spanish **yaya**'s house (the ultimate **yaya** starter kit):

- A Danish cookie tin with sewing supplies inside
- **El gotelé:** a textured wall covering (or stucco) on the wall
- The **sevillana** dancer on top of the TV
- **Los tapetes de ganchillo:** crochet doilies to cover the furniture
- **El abanico:** a handheld fan, as Spanish summers can be tough
- **El porrón:** a Spanish wine pitcher (a traditional vessel used for drinking wine)
- **La pata de jamón y el jamonero:** a cured ham leg and ham holder (stand)
- **La bota de vino:** a wine skin (traditionally a leather bag used to carry wine)

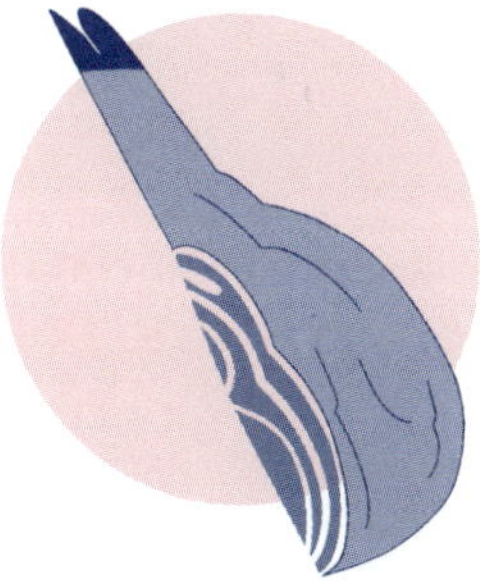

Does your grandma have any of these items!

Or maybe you don't have an **abuela**.

CULTURAL TIP

No tener abuela:
Literally "to not have a grandmother," this is an expression that we use when someone thinks highly of themselves, similarly to how a grandmother would think highly of her grandchild.

MEET THE FAMILY-IN-LAW

Meeting the in-laws can be quite a challenge, especially when you have to start interacting with them on a regular basis.

Brothers-in-law, parents-in-law, stepmother and stepfather... it can all get a bit confusing. And even more so in Spanish, where many words have more than one meaning. Let's go over some key terms that will be useful if you ever marry someone from Spain!

The cuñao

In every family, there is normally a **cuñao**. **What is a cuñao in Spain?**

It means a brother-in-law. However, in informal contexts, **cuñao** describes someone who acts like a know-it-all and gives unsolicited advice, even if they don't really know what they're talking about. This usage is playful and sometimes a bit mocking.

FLUENCY FIX!

REMEMBER, THE CORRECT WORD IS CUÑADO, BUT IN INFORMAL SPEECH, WE USUALLY DON'T PRONOUNCE THE "D" IN WORDS ENDING IN -ADO.

A real **cuñao** thinks his sense of humor is the best and that he is an expert at telling bad jokes (**chistes malos**) and in ordering in bars:

Camarero, tráeme una rubia, pero que no mienta.
Waiter, bring me a blonde [beer], but one that doesn't lie.

He is also an expert at asking for the bill. This is how a real **cuñao** will do it:

*Boss, bring me
the pain.*

And how do you say "stepmother" or "stepfather"?

We have the word **madrastra** or **padrastro**, but these words have negative connotations like **la madrastra** in the Disney movies. These words are old-fashioned.

We say:

la mujer de mi padre
el marido de mi madre
los hijos de mi pareja

We don't say:

la madrastra
el padrastro
los hijastros

I GET ALONG WITH MY FATHER'S WIFE.
ME LLEVO BIEN CON LA MUJER DE MI PADRE.

CULTURAL TIP

Here's a word that doesn't exist in English:

CONSUEGRO/A
It means the father/mother of one's son-in-law
or daughter-in-law.

EATING TONS OF FOOD, FAMILY LUNCH… AND THE SOBREMESA

In Spain, family meals are almost sacred: people eat a lot, drink a lot, and talk even more —sometimes until unexpected hours. Food and the **sobremesa** are practically a religion, and if you haven't experienced it yet, you're missing out on one of the most essential Spanish traditions!

comer vs comerse

If you have a Spanish **yaya** and you go to her house, she will force you to eat until you can't eat anymore, then she will say:

> ¡Cóme**te**lo todo, que
> tienes que crecer!

But why is she using the pronoun **te**? Is it **comer** or **comerse**?

GRAMMAR TIP

With verbs of **ingestion (not with all verbs)** like **beber**, **comer**, **fumar** and **tomar**, we use the pronominal form when there is a specific amount (**uno**, **dos**, **tres**, **todo** and so on) and we want to emphasize that we finish the whole amount.

See these examples:

(Yo) **como** pizza.

(Yo) **me como** una pizza.

(Tú) **tomas** café.

(Tú) **te tomas** 5 cafés.

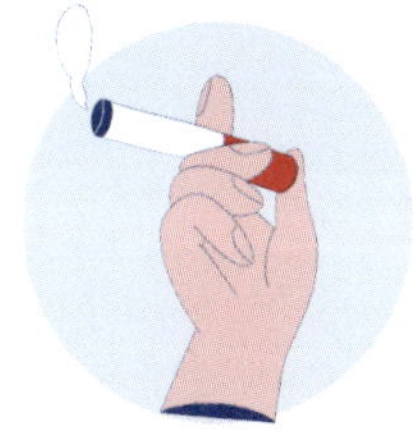

(Él) **fuma** cigarrillos.

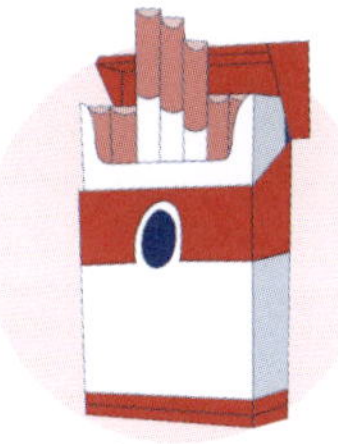

(Él) **se fuma** un paquete al día.

(Nosotros) **bebemos** mucha agua.

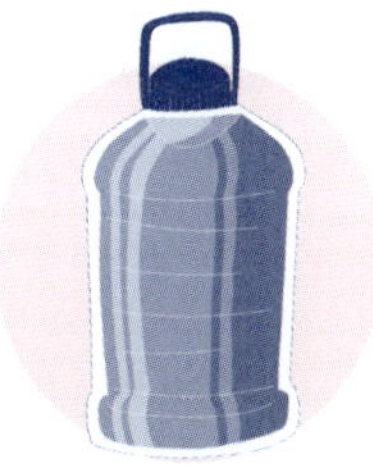

Nos bebemos 2 litros de agua.

You might wonder if it's a mistake not to use the pronoun. It's not, but you will definitely sound more native if you do.

USEFUL SENTENCES DURING A FAMILY MEAL (EN UNA COMIDA FAMILIAR):

Acábatelo todo.
Finish it all. / Eat it all up.

¿Me traes una cerveza?
Can you bring me a beer?

¿Me pasas la sal?
Can you pass me the salt?

¿Me cortas un poco de pan?
Can you cut me a bit of bread?

¿Te pongo un poco más?
Do you want a little more?

¿Alguien quiere repetir?
Does anyone want seconds?

¿Quieres más?
Do you want more?

¿Me das un poco de eso?
Can you give me a bit of that?

Estaba todo buenísimo.
Everything was delicious.

Estoy lleno/a.
I'm full.

How to toast: Cómo brindar

¡Salud!
¡Chinchín!
¡Por nosotros!
¡Por que el Año Nuevo esté lleno de salud, dinero y amor!

And if you want to sound like a native, say this:
Arriba, abajo, al centro y pa dentro.
(Up, down, to the center and in.)

THE SOBREMESA

Once you finish the **primer plato, segundo plato y postre**, you will have a coffee and probably a **chupito** and you will spend many hours around the table talking. This ritual is extremely important in Spanish culture and we even have a word to describe it: the **SOBREMESA**. Sometimes **la sobremesa** will continue after lunch until dinner, though this is more common during special occasions.

8

¡TÍA, TÍA, TÍA!

→ How to master the art of gossiping in Spanish

→ How to react after the gossip

→ Criticize, that guilty pleasure

→ When they want to gossip... but you don't

HOW TO MASTER THE ART OF GOSSIPING IN SPANISH

Some of my favorite activities end in **-eo** and if you don't believe me, just look at these informal terms:

- **El ligoteo:** flirting.
- **El cachondeo:** lighthearted fun, joking or general merrymaking.
- **El bailoteo:** dancing, usually in a casual or carefree way.
- **El tapeo:** a quintessential Spanish activity of going out to eat tapas, typically paired with drinks and socializing.
- **El tardeo:** a newer cultural phenomenon where people enjoy drinks and tapas in the afternoon.
- **El mañaneo:** post-clubbing partying that stretches into the morning hours.
- **El terraceo:** socializing with drinks and possibly food on outdoor terraces, which is very popular in Spain's sunny climate.

And my favorite: **el cotilleo** or **el salseo** or **el chismorreo** (gossiping with your friends).

Sorry, I can't help it (**no lo puedo evitar**). I grew up in the nineties watching Mexican **telenovelas** with my Spanish **abuela**. My favorite one was *María la del Barrio*.

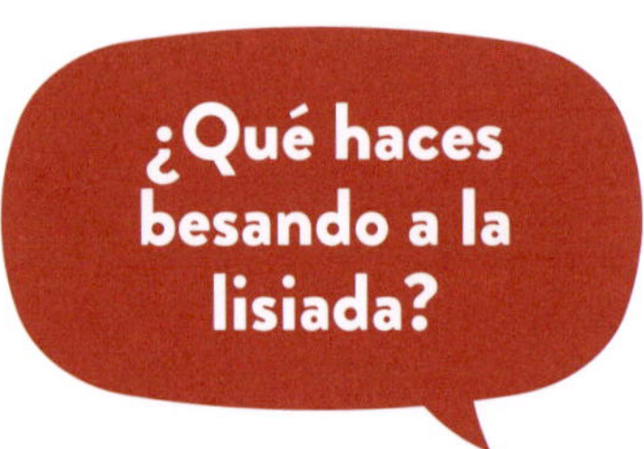

Girlfriends very informally call each other **tía** (aunt). If you say it three times, it means that you have some gossip to share.

The magic word: enterarse

The most important verb that you must know is: **ENTERARSE DE ALGO**. This means to find out about something or to hear about something, depending on the context.

¿Te has enterado de que...? *Did you hear that...?*
Me he enterado de que... *I found out that...*

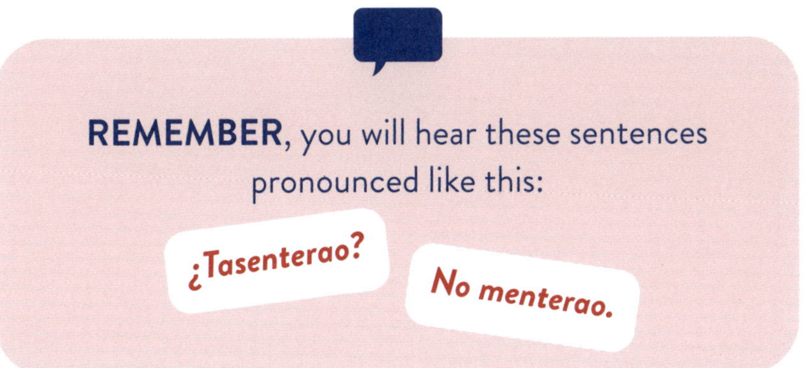

Other sentences that you can use to start gossiping:

Me han contado que...
I've been told that...

He oído que...
I've heard that...

Me ha dicho un pajarito que...
A little bird told me that...

Dicen las malas lenguas que...
Rumor has it that...

Se ve que...
It seems that...

Por lo visto...
Apparently...

Parece ser que...
It appears that...

Resulta que...
It turns out that...

HOW TO REACT AFTER THE GOSSIP

Once you've caught up on the gossip, you can react in several ways: by expressing surprise (or pretending to be surprised), confirming the information, or promising to keep the secret.

How to be very surprised about Spanish gossip:

And the best one: VAYA TELA.

Confirming the information:

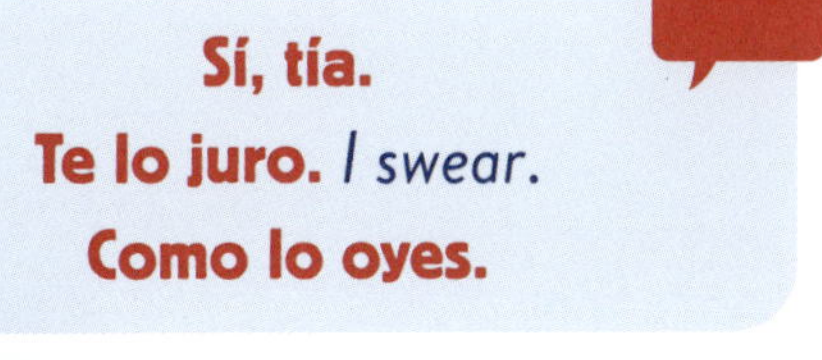

Remember to use a very exaggerated facial expression and body language.

Keeping the secret

After gossiping, you need to make sure that the other person will keep the secret, like this:

No digas nada. *Don't say anything.*

No lo cuentes.

Que no salga de aquí.

Entre tú y yo. *It's between you and me.*

Que quede entre nosotros/as.

Yo no te he dicho nada. *You didn't hear it from me.*

Tranqui, soy una tumba.
I'm a tomb. (Yes, this is our way of saying "My lips are sealed.")

CRITICIZE, THAT GUILTY PLEASURE

The line between gossip and criticism is really thin, and it's also an art you should master if you want to survive in Spain. This is how you can react when others speak badly about someone else.

Now let's criticize people a little so we feel better about ourselves:

ESE PELO LE QUEDA FATAL

Show your agreement:

totalmente / total

tal cual

así es

cien por cien

exacto

ELLA NO TIENE DINERO:

Disagree with a negative sentence:

no ni poco

anda que no

estás tú que no

vaya si no

no ni nada / no ni na

ÉL ES MÁS GUAPO QUE ELLA

Show your disagreement:

qué va

ni de coña (*vulgar*)

para nada

ni de broma

ni mucho menos

nada que ver

And finally: to feel less guilty and better about yourself for gossiping, you can say:

I don't criticize anybody.

Who are we to judge?

And now you can continue with your life...

WHEN THEY WANT TO GOSSIP. . . BUT YOU DON'T

As you can see, gossiping in Spanish can be quite fun, but maybe you won't always be in the mood for it. Let's look at what you can say in these situations to get some peace and quiet.

Hey, by the way (**por cierto**), I also want to know about your life. Tell me about you and you husband. How is it going? I heard he got fired. (**He oído que han despedido a tu marido.**)

Now you are mad. **Ahora estás que sacas humo por las orejas**. Of course it was more fun talking about other people:

If you are in a situation like this, you can say...

No es asunto tuyo.
No es tu problema.
No te concierne.
Esto no te incumbe.
No te metas donde no te llaman.
Eso no va contigo.
¿Y a ti qué te importa?

All these sentences mean the same:

It's none of your business

Unwanted opinions

Sometimes you tell a friend something just to vent, but you don't always get the response you want.

He vuelto a quedar con Juan. Sé que no se ha portado demasiado bien conmigo, pero creo que se merece otra oportunidad. Pero no lo cuentes, ¿eh? Nadie lo sabe.
I've met up with Juan again. I know he hasn't been very good to me, but I think he deserves another chance. But don't tell it, huh? Nobody knows.

Types of responses you can expect in a situation like this:

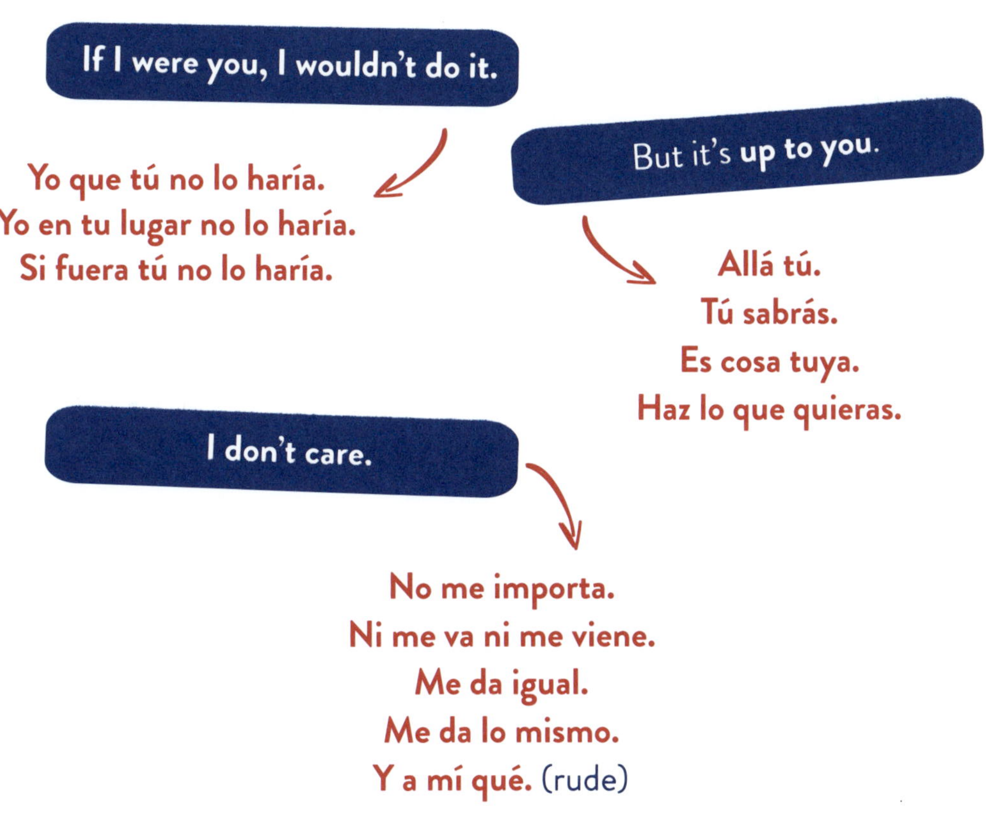

In Spanish, we have one thousand rude ways to say "I don't care." Any of these will do:

ME IMPORTA UN:

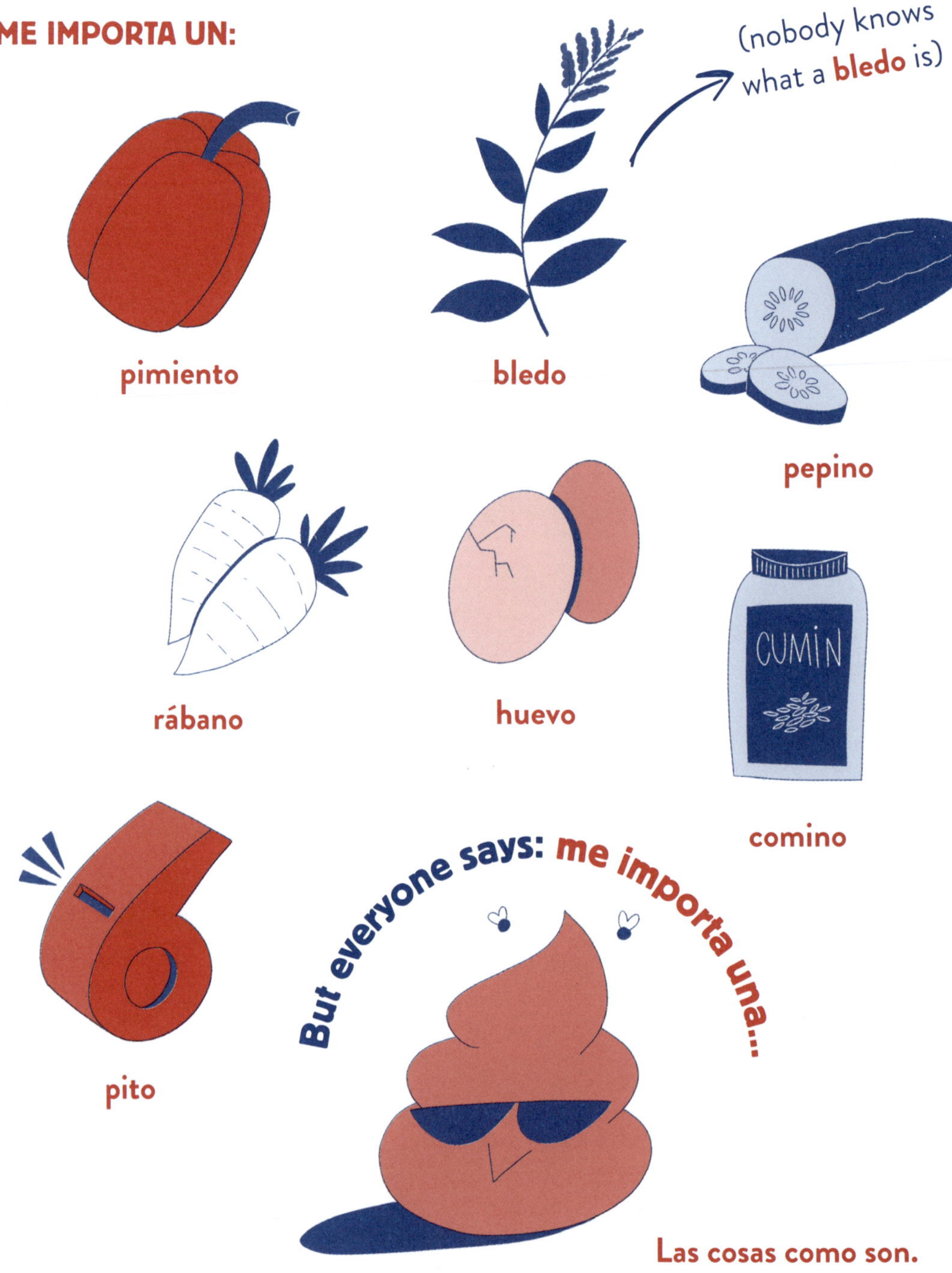

9

→ Useful words in class

→ The Spanish school system

→ Being good or bad at something

→ Student problems

USEFUL WORDS IN CLASS

In class, many objects are used. Let's go over some of the most common ones so you can familiarize yourself with the vocabulary. I'm sure it will be useful in any setting, even at work!

CLASSROOM ESSENTIALS

pizarra *board*
tiza *chalk*
borrador *eraser* (**para la pizarra**)
goma de borrar *eraser* (**para lápiz**)
rotulador *marker*
cuaderno-libreta *notebook*
libro de texto *textbook*
carpeta *folder*
escritorio *desk*
mochila *backpack*
tijeras *scissors*
pegamento *glue*
calculadora *calculator*
grapadora *stapler*
clips *paper clips*
chinchetas *push pins*
regla *ruler*
compás *compass*
estuche *pencil case*

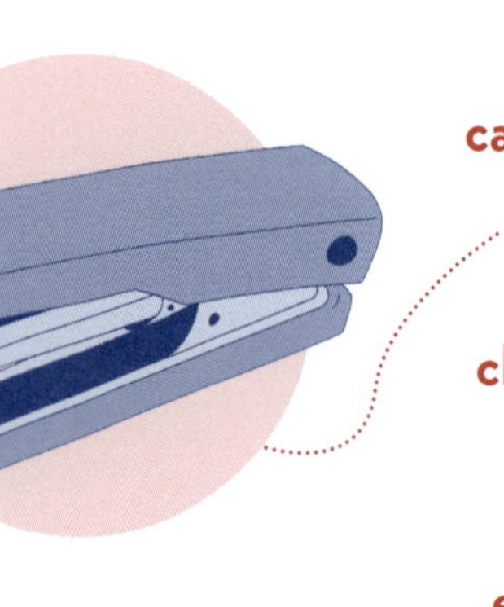

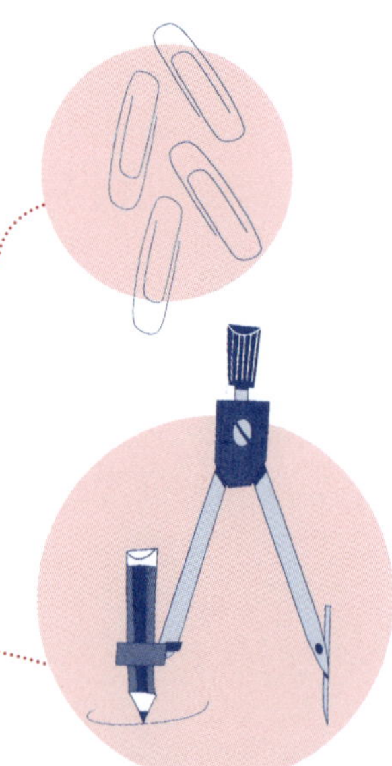

¡Nos falta algo? (Are we missing something?): _______________

Notice something important: We call our teachers by their name (María, Luis, etc.) or just **profe**. The relationship is often informal and more friendly than in Anglo-Saxon cultures.

In the nineties, it wasn't like that. We used to say *Señorita* María and *Don* Antonio, but that was very old school. Yes, I'm a millennial.

YOU MAY HAVE ALREADY NOTICED THAT WE SHORTEN MANY WORDS IN SPANISH:

universidad:
uni
university

colegio:
cole
school

instituto:
insti
high school / secondary school

guardería:
guarde
daycare

profesor:
profe
teacher

director:
dire
principal

compañero:
compi
classmate

bolígrafo:
boli
pen

autobús:
bus
bus

bicicleta:
bici
bike

oposiciones:
opos
public service exams

biblioteca:
biblio
library

matemáticas:
mates
mathematics

filosofía:
filo
philosophy

facultad:
facu
faculty

AHORA TÚ:

fin de semana: _______________

por favor: _______________

película: _______________

peluquería: _______________

supermercado: _______________

televisión: _______________

policía: _______________

oficina: _______________

cumpleaños: _______________

Soluciones: finde, porfa, peli, pelu, súper, tele, poli, ofi, cumple.

124

THE SPANISH SCHOOL SYSTEM

The Spanish education system is divided into several stages, starting with **infantil** (**guardería**) for young children, followed by **primaria** (primary school) for ages 6 to 12. After primary school, students move on to **secundaria** (secondary school), which is divided into **obligatoria** (compulsory) and **bachillerato** (high school), leading to **universidad** (university), or **formación profesional** (vocational training).

Voy a la GUARDERÍA.
Tengo 5 meses.

Voy al COLEGIO.
Tengo 6 años.

Voy al INSTITUTO.
Tengo 15 años.

Voy a la UNIVERSIDAD.
Tengo 20 años.

guardería: from 0 to 3 years old
preescolar: from 3 to 6 years old
primaria: from 6 to 12 years old
instituto/secundaria: from 12 to 16 years old
bachillerato: from 16 to 18 years old (pre-university)
universidad: from 18 years old

A classic in every class: el empollón (the nerd)

I'm sure there was someone like this in your high school. They say things like this:

Nunca me he hecho una **chuleta**.
I've never made a cheat sheet.

Estudio **hasta las tantas**.
I study until late at night.

Nunca me **pillan** copiando.
They never catch me cheating.

Les hago la **pelota** a los profes.
I suck up to the teachers.

Saco buenas **notas** en todo.
I get good grades in everything.

Nunca he **suspendido** un examen.
I've never failed an exam.

Nunca he **faltado** a clase.
I've never skipped class.

Ningún profe **me tiene manía**.
No teacher has it in for me.

Siempre **tomo apuntes**.
I always take notes.

Be careful with these informal terms:

NORMAL MEANING	INFORMAL MEANING
una chuleta	**una chuleta**

chop	*cheat sheet*

una pelota	**un/una pelota**

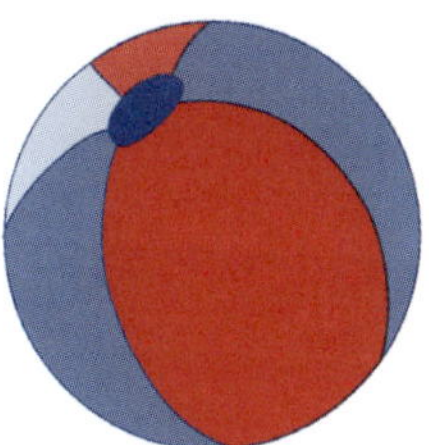

ball	*brown-noser*

un rollo	**un rollo**

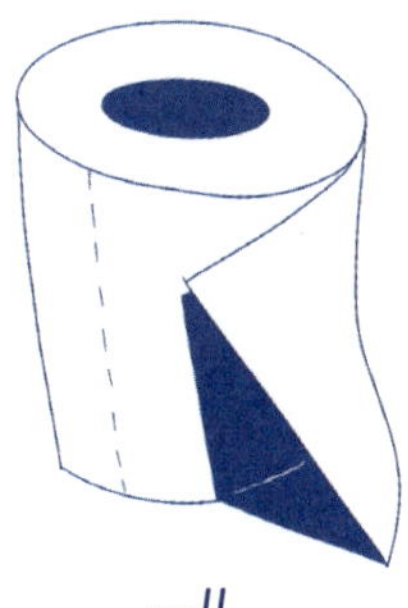

roll	*something boring*

BEING GOOD OR BAD AT SOMETHING

When I was a kid, I was bad at math. **Cuando era pequeña, se me daban mal las mates.** To say that you're good or bad at something, you can say **soy bueno para eso** or **soy malo para esto**, but we do have better options:

Se me da bien/genial.
Tengo facilidad para...
Domino este tema.
Soy un/a crack.
Soy un/a fiera.

Soy un/a máquina.
Soy un coco.
Soy lo más.
Soy el/la mejor.

And a response you can expect if you say this...

Eres un **flipado**.
You've got a big head.

Se me da mal/fatal.
Soy un negado / una
    negada para...
Soy un/a desastre para...

No es mi fuerte.
No es lo mío.
No me entero.
No lo pillo.

FLUENCY FIX!

✗ Instead of saying **es muy difícil para mí**,
you will sound more natural if you say:

✔ **Me resulta muy difícil.**
✔ **Me cuesta mucho.**

And what are you good at? Traditionally, students have been divided into those who focus on science and those who focus on the humanities. Which one do you identify with?

SOY DE CIENCIAS.

I'm more into science.

símbolos matemáticos

+	suma (más)
−	resta (menos)
× o ·	multiplicación (por)
÷ o /	división (entre)
=	igual
<	menor que
>	mayor que
√	raíz cuadrada
%	porcentaje

SOY DE LETRAS.

I'm more into the humanities.

signos de puntuación

.	punto	" " o « »	comillas
,	coma	( )	paréntesis
;	punto y coma	[ ]	corchetes
:	dos puntos	-	guion
…	puntos suspensivos	—	raya
¿?	signos de interrogación	/	barra
¡!	signos de exclamación		

THE MOST COMMON FEAR WHILE STUDYING: THE GRADES

In Spain, grades (**las notas**) go from 0 to 10, with 0 being the worst and 10 being the best.

insuficiente: 0-5
suficiente: 5
bien: 6
notable: 7-8
sobresaliente: 9-10

Useful sentences:

¿Qué nota has sacado?
What grade did you get?
¿Has aprobado o suspendido?
Did you pass or fail?
He aprobado. He sacado un 7.
I have approved. I got a 7.
Tengo que repetir el examen.
I have to take the test again.

In some Spanish-speaking countries, people use the expression **pasar el examen** because of English influence.

STUDENT PROBLEMS

When I was a kid, I usually got bored in class. In Spain we say: I get bored like an oyster. Don't ask me why, but it kind of makes sense. Just look at this:

Another very big problem that I had when I was a teenager was that I'm not a morning person. **No soy una persona mañanera** and I hate waking up early in the morning. In Spanish, we have a specific verb for that:

> MADRUGAR

I'm a night owl (**soy una persona nocturna**) and I like to pull all-nighters. **Me gusta trasnochar.**

> TRASNOCHAR

Are you **mañanero/a** or **nocturno/a**?

That's why I always fell asleep in class.
(Siempre me dormía en las clases.)

PAY ATTENTION TO THE DIFFERENCES:

dormir *to sleep*

Duermo poco.

dormir**se** *to fall asleep*

Me duermo en clase.

Here are more verbs that change their meaning if they have **se**:

despedir
to fire

ir
to go

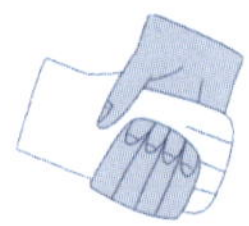

quedar
to meet up

llevar
to carry

acordar
to agree on something

encontrar
to find

llamar
to call

despedir**se**
to say goodbye

ir**se**
to leave

quedar**se**
to stay

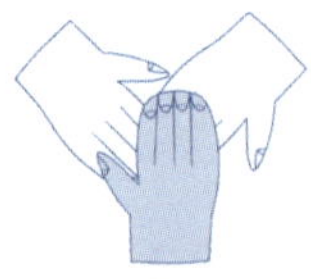

llevar**se**
to get along

acordar**se**
to remember

encontrar**se**
to find oneself

llamar**se**
to be called

AND A FINAL QUESTIONNAIRE:

¿Eres más de ciencias o de letras?
Are you more into science or the humanities?

____

¿Qué asignaturas se te daban bien en el colegio?
Which subjects were you good at in school?

____

¿Qué notas sacabas en el instituto?
What grades did you get in high school?

____

¿Alguna vez suspendiste un examen?
Did you ever fail an exam?

____

¿Alguna vez te hiciste una chuleta?
Did you ever make a cheat sheet?

____

¿Quién era el empollón de tu clase?
Who was the nerd in your class?

____

¿Para qué cosas eres negado?
What things are you bad at?

____

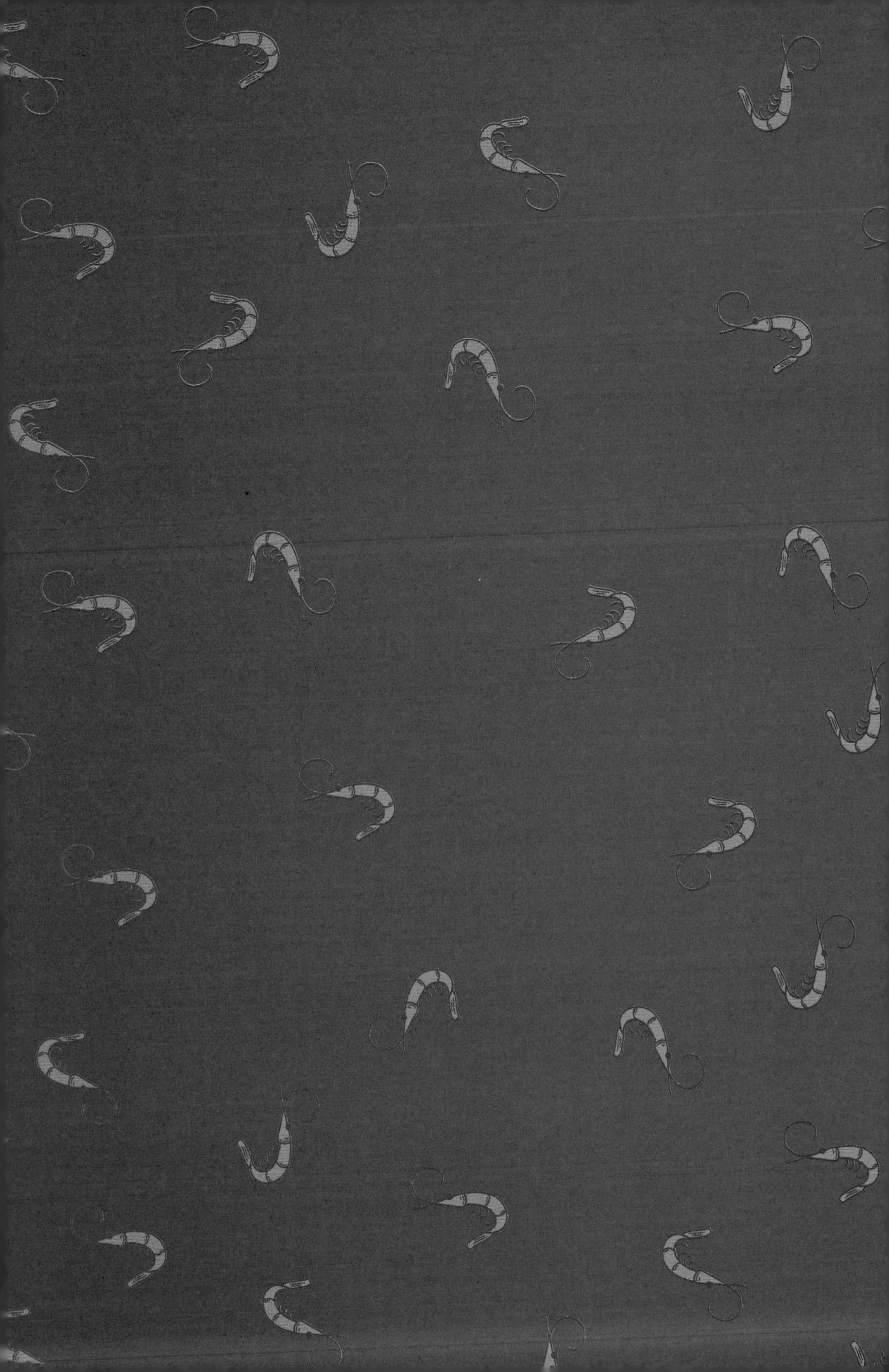

10

ME TOCA CURRAR

- → Tell me about your job
- → Vocabulary related to work (adults only)
- → The **compis**
- → How to interact in the work WhatsApp group
- → Useful sentences for a video call
- → How to write a formal email
- → Finally Friday

TELL ME ABOUT YOUR JOB

¿Qué querías ser de pequeño?

Everybody says that you have to earn a living (ganarse la vida), and that's why it's important to find a calling (tu vocación).

My calling has always been to help people. I've always wanted to be a lawyer.

What are you talking about, Mari? When you were little, you wanted to be a YouTuber.

Yo de pequeño/a quería ser:

____

What's your job?

Yo soy **funcionaria** y ahora estoy de baja por maternidad y no sé cuándo me **reincorporaré**. Quizá me pillo una **excedencia**.
I'm a civil servant and right now I'm on maternity leave. I don't know when I'll return to work. Maybe I'll take a leave of absence.

Trabajo en una oficina y estoy **quemado**. Tengo un **contrato temporal**. Hago mil horas extras y me pagan la mitad de mi sueldo en negro. **No llego a fin de mes**.
I work in an office and I'm burned out. I have a temporary contract. I do a thousand hours of overtime and they pay me half my salary under the table. I can't make ends meet.

Yo soy un **vividor**. **No doy un palo al agua**. Ahora estoy **en el paro** y luego **ya se verá**.
I'm a freeloader. I won't lift a finger. Right now I'm collecting unemployment and we'll see what happens next.

Yo soy un **trepa**. Solo busco **ascender** de manera deshonesta, **a costa** de otras personas. *I'm a social climber. I only seek to rise in a dishonest way, at the expense of others.*

Yo soy **autónoma**. Pago una barbaridad de impuestos. *I'm self-employed, I pay a huge amount of taxes.*

Y TÚ, ¡A QUÉ TE DEDICAS?

¿Te gusta tu trabajo?

¿En qué industria trabajas?

¿Cuál es tu puesto?

VOCABULARY RELATED TO WORK (ADULTS ONLY)

jornada laboral
working hours

declaración de la renta
income tax return

jubilación
retirement / pension

impuestos taxes

plan de pensiones
pension plan

préstamo loan

hipoteca
mortgage

inversiones
investments

facturas
invoices / bills

nómina
payslip / paycheck

ahorrar to save

baja laboral
sick leave / medical leave

cobrar
to earn / to receive (payment)

estar en paro
to be unemployed / to be out of work

despido improcedente
wrongful termination

trabajo a tiempo completo
full time job

trabajo a tiempo parcial
part-time job

sueldo wage

salario salary

CULTURAL TIP

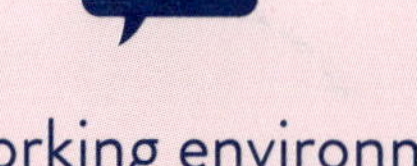

In Spanish working environments,
you can hear things like:

Mañana **me toca** currar hasta las tantas.
It's my turn to… / I have to…

In Spain, the work environment can be more informal
compared to some other countries, particularly in
the tech industry, the media and creative fields.
Spanish people tend to have a direct communication
style and it's common to use informal language
even with superiors, especially in more relaxed work
environments or smaller companies.

Standard vs informal vocabulary at work

STANDARD SPANISH

trabajar *to work*
el trabajo *the job*
muy trabajador *very hardworking*
dinero *money*
estar cansado *to be tired*
ser rico *to be rich*

no tener dinero *to have no money*
no tener tiempo *to have no time*
estar muy ocupado *to be very busy*
tener mucho trabajo *to have a lot
of work*
hasta muy tarde *until very late*

currar *to grind*
el curro *the job*
currante/a *workhorse*
pasta *dough*
estar reventado *to be shattered*
estar forrado *to be loaded*
no tener ni un duro *to be broke*

no darme la vida
 to be overwhelmed
estar liado *to be tied up*
estar a tope de curro
 to have a full plate
hasta las tantas
 until the early hours

FLUENCY FIX!

As you may have noticed, in Spanish many
verbs are used, and the shift from formal to informal
usage happens very quickly.

For example, to say you're really tired, the verb
reventar is used, which means "to burst."
I know, strange, right? **Spanish is wonderful!**

**Hoy estoy reventado, he currado
hasta las tantas.**

THE COMPIS

A colleague in Spain is a compañero de trabajo, also known by the shorter, informal version: compi.

This is how you can ask your colleague for a favor:
¿Me harías un favor?
Necesito un favor.
¿Me haces un favor/favorcito? (If you add **-ito** to any word
it will sound nicer.)
¿Puedo pedirte un favor?
¿Me ayudarías en algo?

They can answer according to this:
Si tienes un compi guay *If you have a cool colleague:*
por supuesto
faltaría más
dame un segundo y estoy contigo
claro que sí
ahora mismo

Si tu compi no mola *If your colleague is not cool:*
es que ahora no puedo
estoy muy liado/a
me pillas a punto de salir
luego si eso ya lo vemos (remember this means "no.")

HOW TO INTERACT IN THE WORK WHATSAPP GROUP

The theory is great, but sometimes it's better to see things put into practice, right? Let's look at some examples of useful conversations at work so you can have it all clear.

Making an appointment:

¿Cuál es tu disponibilidad?
Dime **cuándo te iría mejor** /
Dime cuándo podrías.

El martes me va bien.

Vale, agendado.

Canceling an appointment:

Buenos días, por motivos personales me veo obligado/a a cancelar nuestra cita de hoy; ¿sería posible **aplazarla**?

No te preocupes, **lo dejamos para** la semana que viene.

Muchas gracias por tu comprensión; hasta la próxima semana.

Tranquilo/a, no hay problema.

Following up (hacer un seguimiento):

Hola! Te escribo para saber cuándo podrías tener los documentos que te pedí. Es que **me corre un poquito de prisa**.

Ahora mismo estoy ocupada, pero te lo miro **en cuanto pueda y te digo algo**.

Vale, no hay problema; **avísame** en cuanto lo tengas.

Buenos días, Julián: **Todavía no he recibido la transferencia, ¿va todo bien?**

Ah, pues la realizamos la semana pasada, debería haberte llegado.

Qué raro, **es posible** que no la haya visto.

Te agredecería que me lo confirmaras. Un abrazo.

Vale, **lo miro y te escribo** dentro de un rato.

USEFUL SENTENCES FOR A VIDEO CALL

Video calls are here to stay, and they're being used more and more in the daily routine of many jobs. If you live in Spain and work for a Spanish company, chances are you'll spend your day in front of a screen attending meetings. Let's go over the most important things so you can survive your day-to-day!

No te oigo bien, disculpa. *Sorry, I can't hear you well.*

Hay mucho ruido de fondo. *There is a lot of background noise.*

Se corta la conexión. *The connection is cutting out.*

Internet va muy lento. *The Internet is very slow.*

Tu micrófono está en silencio. *Your microphone is muted.*

¿Podrías subir/bajar el volumen? *Could you turn the volume up/down?*

No te veo, ¿podrías encender la cámara? *I can't see you. Could you turn on the camera?*

La pantalla se ha quedado congelada. *The screen is frozen.*

Voy a reiniciar el equipo. *I'm going to restart the computer.*

Voy a intentar conectarme de nuevo. *I'm going to try reconnecting.*

Voy a compartir mi pantalla. *I'm going to share my screen.*

HOW TO WRITE A FORMAL EMAIL

Even if we are generally informal, sometimes it's necessary to be very formal.

Nos ponemos serios. Let's send a formal email:

querido/a *dear*

estimado/a *dear/esteemed*

Me pongo en contacto contigo para... *I am reaching out to you to...*

Te escribo para... *I am writing to...*

Me gustaría hacerte una propuesta. *I would like to make you a proposal.*

Nos gustaría contar contigo para... *We would like to have you for...*

Sería un placer colaborar contigo. *It would be a pleasure to work together with you.*

Te adjunto los documentos que me pediste. *I have attached the documents you requested.*

Quedo a la espera de tu respuesta. *I look forward to your response.*

Quedo a tu disposición. *I remain at your disposal.*

atentamente *sincerely*

un cordial saludo *kind regards*

FINALLY FRIDAY

¡Por fin es viernes! ¡Aunque prefiero el juernes!

The Spanish slang word **juernes** is used to refer to the feeling that Thursday is like Friday, especially when people are eager for the weekend. It describes the excitement or the early start of weekend-like activities on Thursday.

Pero este finde no voy a salir porque soy un *viejoven*

This slang word describes someone who is in their 20s or early 30s, but acts like someone in their 40s: still young, but behaving like an older person who doesn't want to go to clubs, party, drink, etc., but prefers spending the weekend at home watching movies on the sofa.

11

TE SIGO EN REDES

⟶ Phone related vocabulary and useful sentences

⟶ How to chat with your friends in Spanish

⟶ Basic vocabulary for social media

⟶ English words we use with a different meaning

⟶ Vocabulary basics: **Onomatopoeias** and Spanish sounds

PHONE RELATED VOCABULARY AND USEFUL SENTENCES

Has your mom, dad or anyone else in your family ever said this to you?

Estás todo el día mirando el dichoso móvil.
You're on that damn phone all day.

Estás enganchada/o a esa cosa.
You're addicted to that thing.

Se te va a quedar la cara cuadrada de tanta pantalla.
You're going to get square eyes from all that screen time.

Well, they're right. We are all addicted to our phones. **Yo también.**

Useful sentences while using your phone

Now let's talk about your phone.

Notice that in Spain we say **el móvil** and in most Spanish-speaking countries they say **el celular**.

encender el móvil *turn on the phone*
apagar el móvil *turn off the phone*
subir el volumen *raise the volume*
bajar el volumen *lower the volume*
mandar un mensaje *send a message*

recibir un mensaje
receive a message
borrar un mensaje
delete a message
dejar en visto *leave on read*

More useful sentences:

Tengo batería baja.
My battery is low.

Se me ha acabado la batería.
My battery has run out.

Se me ha apagado el móvil. *My phone has turned off.*

Se me ha muerto el móvil. *My phone died.*

Necesito cargar el móvil.
I need to charge my phone.

¿Tienes un cargador? *Do you have a charger?*

¿Dónde hay un enchufe? *Where is a socket?*

No tengo cobertura.
I have no coverage.

No da señal. *There's no signal.*

Comunica. *The line is busy.*

No lo coge. *He/she isn't answering.*

Llamo y no contesta.
I'm calling him/her, but he/she isn't answering.

151

HOW TO CHAT WITH YOUR FRIENDS IN SPANISH

Spanish **slang** that you must know to understand your Spanish friends, especially if you use social media:

no quiero: **paso** *I don't want*

no te preocupes: **no te rayes** *don't worry*

me voy: **me piro / me largo** *I'm leaving*

la gente: **la peña** *people*

estoy muy sorprendido: **flipo / qué fuerte / qué heavy** *that's crazy*

me parece mal: **vaya tela** *what a mess*

por ejemplo: **en plan** *I mean*

me gusta: **me mola** *I like it*

me gusta mucho: **me flipa** *I love it*

bonito: **guay** *nice, cool*

es increíble: **es una pasada / es lo más** *it's incredible*

qué aburrido: **qué rollo / qué coñazo**
how boring / what a drag

amiga: **tía** *girl*

amigo: **bro** *friend*

estás loco: **se te va la olla** *you're crazy*

And of course, these four words:

cutre *shabby*
hortera *kitschy, tacky*
majo *friendly*
borde *unfriendly, rude*

CORNY EXPRESSIONS IN SPANISH

Some expressions that we use a lot with our friends, but can make you cringe if you are intolerant to sugar:

NORMAL SPANISH

cariño

hola

hasta luego

besos

amigo

por favor

guapa

CORNY SPANISH ESPAÑOL CURSI

cari

holi

hasta luegui

besis

amigui

porfi/porfis

guapi

CULTURAL TIP

In Spain, waiters, shop assistants, or even hairdressers might use these expressions with you, regardless of whether they know you well, so don't worry if this happens to you! Welcome to Spain, I guess.

BASIC VOCABULARY FOR SOCIAL MEDIA

If you're anything like me, you probably have your phone glued to your hand. Social media is part of our daily lives, and knowing how to navigate its language is important, both professionally and personally. Getting a DM, following someone, or liking a friend's post feels completely natural and almost automatic, but how do you say it in Spanish?

seguir
to follow

dejar de seguir
to unfollow

bloquear
to block

guardar
to save

etiquetar
to tag

compartir
to share

darle like
to like

publicar / subir un post
to post

seguidores
followers

comentar
to comment

enviar mensaje directo *to send a direct message (DM)*

deslizar *to scroll / swipe*

iniciar sesión
log in

cerrar sesión
log out

poner la contraseña
insert password

EL POSTUREO

I really like social media as a way to connect with people and discover new opportunities (new friends, a new job and maybe a new love). But one thing I don't like is **EL POSTUREO**.

El **postureo** en redes sociales es increíble.
The posing on social media is unbelievable.

Postureo is a slang term that refers to the act of trying to appear in a certain way to impress others, often superficially and exaggeratedly. It's about showing off, posturing or pretending to be something you're not.

SPANISH SLANG IN SOCIAL MEDIA BASED IN ANGLICISMS

In Spanish, we use a lot of anglicisms and we adapt them to our conjugation. Look at these words:

wasapear (mandar un wasap)
to send a WhatsApp message

Luego te wasapeo cuando llegue.
I'll WhatsApp you when I get there.

postear (publicar)
to post on social media

Voy a postear la foto del viaje.
I'm going to post the photo from the trip.

stalkear (espiar) *to stalk*

Estuve stalkeando su perfil, y parece que le gusta viajar.
I was stalking their profile, and it looks like they like to travel.

chatear (hablar con alguien por redes sociales) *to chat*

Pasamos la tarde chateando en Instagram.
We spent the afternoon chatting on Instagram.

spamear (enviar contenido molesto repetidamente) *to spam*

Deja de spamear el grupo con memes.
Stop spamming the group with memes.

banear (bloquear) *to ban*

**Me banearon por usar un programa
externo en el juego.** *I got banned for using
an external program in the game.*

hacer scroll (deslizar)
to scroll

Pasé horas haciendo scroll en *TikTok*.
I spent hours scrolling through TikTok.

hacer un live (transmitir contenido en directo)
to broadcast a livestream

Voy a hacer un live para hablar de la receta.
I'm going to broadcast a livestream to talk about the recipe.

hacer swipe (deslizar) *to swipe*

Si no te gusta, haz swipe a la izquierda.
If you don't like him, swipe left.

hacer click *to click*

Solo tienes que hacer click aquí para descargarlo.
You just have to click here to download it.

darle like (darle me gusta) *to like a post on social media*

Le di like a tu publicación.
I liked your post.

WHAT ABOUT YOU?
DO YOU LIKE THE POSTUREO?
It's time to practice your Spanish!

¿Qué tipo de contenido subes a redes?
What kind of content do you post on social media?

____

____

¿Cuánto rato pasas en redes sociales al día?
How much time do you spend on social media per day?

____

____

¿Qué tipo de cuentas sigues?
What kind of accounts do you follow?

____

____

¿Te gusta más postear o stalkear?
Do you prefer posting or stalking?

____

____

ENGLISH WORDS WE USE WITH A DIFFERENT MEANING

As you can see, we use a lot of English words in Spanish, but sometimes we change their original meaning and adapt them to what we think they mean. Look at these examples:

Esta chica es muy **fashion**.

This girl is very fashionable.

Me da buen **feeling** y además es una **crack**.

She gives me good vibes and is also awesome.

Other English words that are not used in English like we use them in Spanish.

puenting *bungee jumping*	**footing** *jogging*	**esmoquin** *from "smoking jacket": tuxedo*
zapping *channel surfing*	**body** *tight top*	**mobbing** *workplace harassment*
friki *weirdo*	**lifting** *face lift*	**camping** *campground*

...ay, this is not ...en English (lol).

VOCABULARY BASICS: ONOMATOPOEIAS AND SPANISH SOUNDS

Onomatopoeias and sounds are different in Spanish. Here you have sounds that Spanish people make:

Achoo

Onomatopoeia for a sneeze

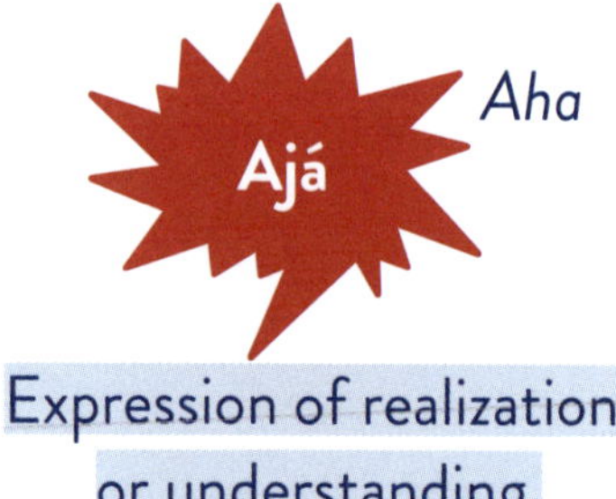

Aha

Expression of realization or understanding

Ouch/Oh

Expression of pain or surprise

Shh

To ask for silence or get someone's attention quietly

Ahem

To clear the throat or subtly hint at something

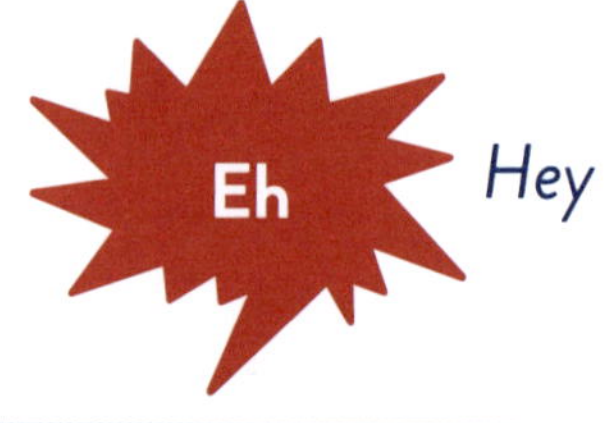

Hey

To call someone or express surprise

Wow/Whoa

Expression of astonishment or encouragement

Oops/Whoa

Expression of surprise or fright

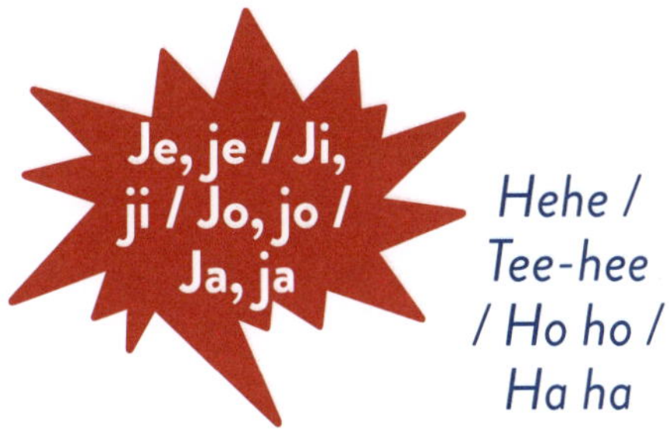

Hehe / Tee-hee / Ho ho / Ha ha

Laughter in different tones

Yum yum

Used for eating or delicious food

Mwah

Kissing sound

Plop

The sound of something falling

Yuck/Ew

Expression of disgust

Phew

Expression of relief or exhaustion

Oops/Whoa

Expression of warning or surprise

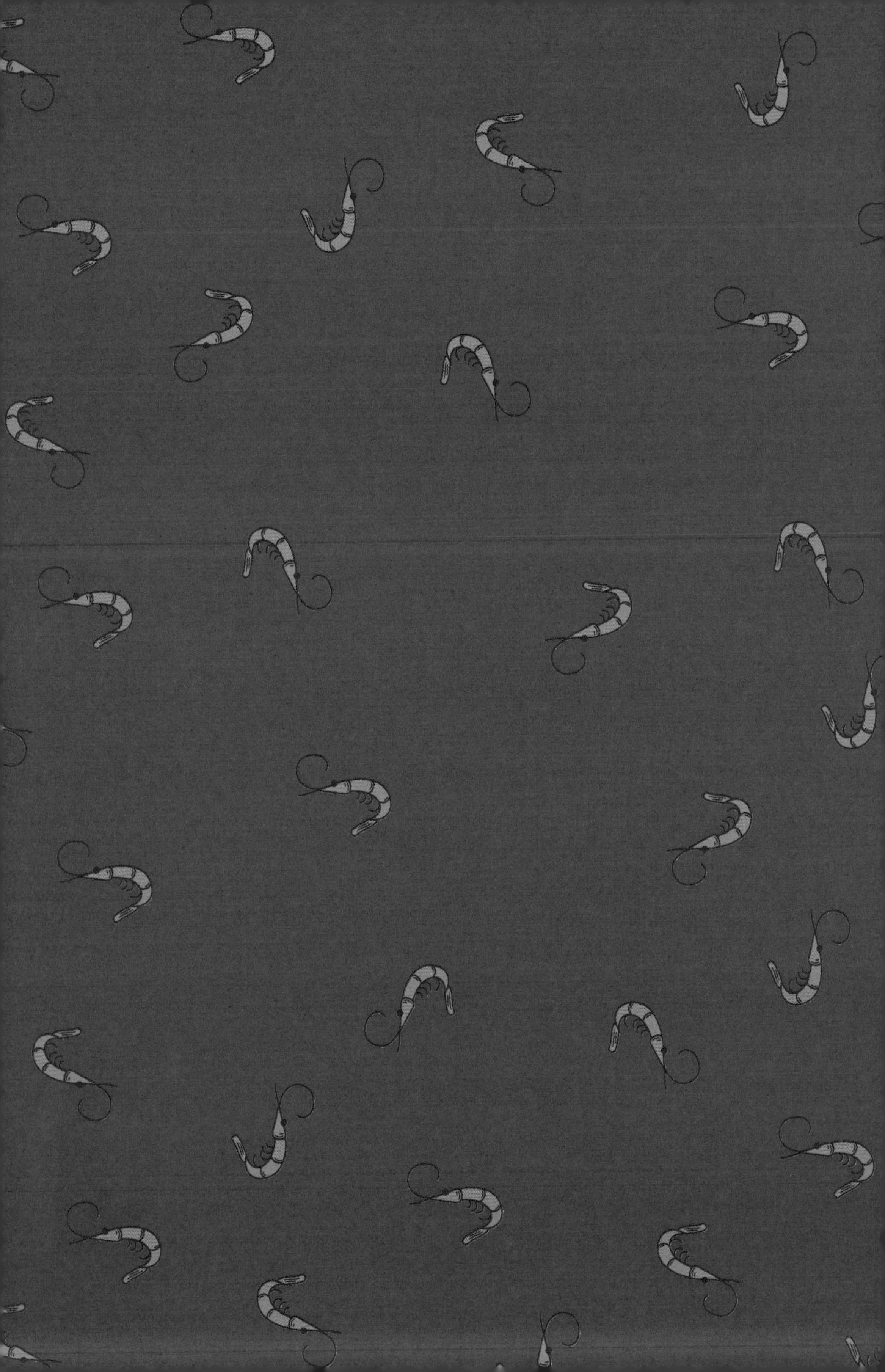

12

VAYA PINTAS

REMEMBER: YOU ARE BEAUTIFUL

Body appearance and self-care are very important. Comb your hair, apply creams, and, above all, take care of your skin. Below, you'll find practical vocabulary so you can always be at your best (or know how to ask for help if you need it).

Pintas is a slang word that refers to someone's appearance or look, especially when it's unusual, messy or not very presentable. It's often used in a casual or humorous way to comment on how someone looks, sometimes critically or playfully.

We also use it to talk about the appearance of food:
qué buena pinta / qué mala pinta *it looks good / it looks bad*

Now it's time to talk about beauty and selfcare.

First of all, let's normalize having these:

ojeras *dark circles under the eyes*

bolsas *bags*

arrugas *wrinkles*

granos *pimples*

papada *double chin*

manchas *spots (or blemishes)*

rojeces *redness*

caspa *dandruff*

estrías *stretch marks*

celulitis *cellulite*

cicatrices *scars*

lunares *moles*

pecas *freckles*

In case nobody told you today, your skin is beautiful and you are perfect just the way you are. **Even so, it's understandable that you want to look your best.**

¡VAMOS A HABLAR DE ELLO A CONTINUACIÓN!

HAIR ISSUES

La longitud del pelo *Hair length*

pelo largo *long hair*
media melena *medium-length hair*
pelo corto *short hair*
rapado *buzz cut*
pelo hasta los hombros *shoulder-length hair*
pelo hasta la cintura *waist-length hair*

Tipos de peinados

PELO SUELTO
loose hair

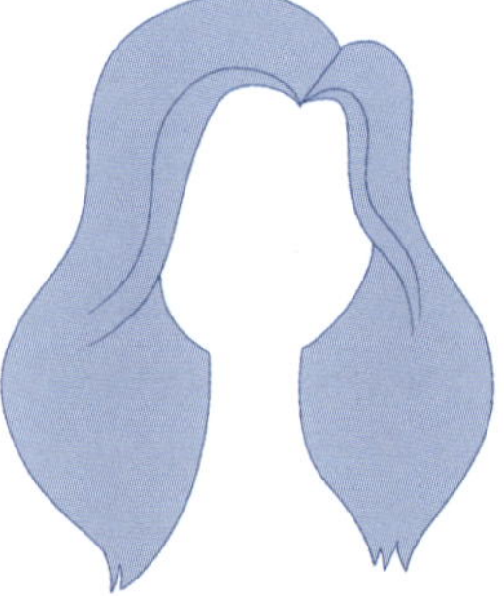

PELO RECOGIDO
updo

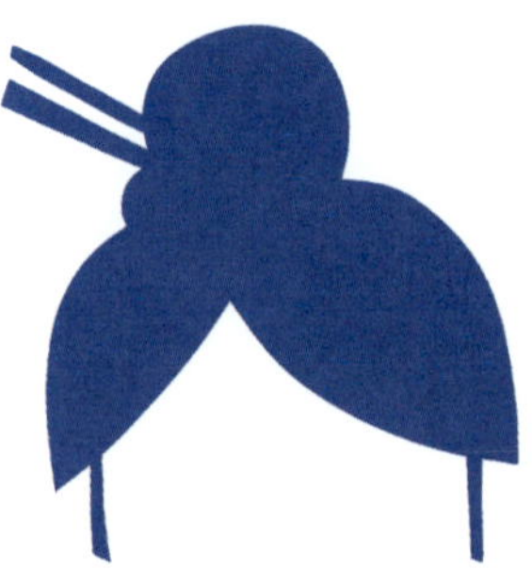

RAYA AL MEDIO
middle part
COLETA
ponytail
TRENZA
braid
MOÑO
bun
MOÑO ALTO
high bun

RAYA AL LADO
side part
DOS COLETAS
pigtails
DOS TRENZAS
pigtail braids
MOÑO DESPEINADO
messy bun
MOÑO BAJO
low bun

I have an existential question. Why does the shampoo label always insult me?

PARA PELO FINO, GRASO, POBRE, MALTRATADO, CASTIGADO
For fine, oily, weak, damaged, over-processed hair

"I just wanted it for dirty hair."

FOR BETTER OR WORSE, THERE ARE MANY TYPES OF HAIR (TIPOS DE PELO).
¿Cómo es el tuyo?

pelo liso/lacio *straight hair* ☐

pelo ondulado *wavy hair* ☐

pelo rizado *curly hair* ☐

pelo afro *afro-textured hair* ☐

pelo crespo *coiled/kinky hair* ☐

pelo grueso *thick hair* ☐

pelo fino *thin/delicate/fine hair* ☐

pelo seco *dry hair* ☐

pelo graso *oily hair* ☐

pelo teñido *dyed hair* ☐

pelo canoso *hair with gray strands / "gray hair"* ☐

USEFUL SENTENCES AT THE HAIR SALON AND BARBERSHOP

Ready to take on the challenge of booking a hair salon appointment? Don't worry, it's not as complicated as it seems, even though it might feel like a real task at times! In this chapter, I'll guide you on how to do it easily and with style. Get ready to talk cuts and let your hair shine.

Hola, buenas. ¿Tienes hora para cortarme el pelo mañana?

Hello, good morning. Do you have time available for me to get a haircut tomorrow?

Sí. ¿a qué hora te va bien? ¿A las 4?

Yes. What time works for you? At 4?

¿A las 5:30, puede ser? Es que a las 4 no puedo.

How about 5:30? I can't make it at 4.

Vale, pues a las 5.30.

Okay then, at 5.30.

¿Qué te vas a hacer?

What do you want to do?

Cortarme las puntas y hacerme unas mechas.

Just trim the ends and get some highlights.

Muy bien, pues ya estás apuntada. Hasta mañana.

All right, you're booked. See you tomorrow.

REQUESTING A HAIRCUT (PEDIR UN CORTE DE PELO)

Quiero cortarme el pelo.
I want a haircut.

Solo quiero las puntas, por favor.
I just want the ends trimmed, please.

Quiero un cambio de look.
I want a makeover.

¿Puedes hacerme este corte?
Can you give me this haircut?

No lo cortes demasiado, por favor.
Don't cut it too short, please.

Quiero hacerme un flequillo.
I want bangs.

And that awkward moment when the hairdresser asks you if you liked it?

In the barbershop (En la barbería)

COMMON SERVICES AT THE BARBER SHOP:

recortar la barba *trim my beard*
perfilar la barba *shape my beard*
afeitar la barba completamente *shave my beard off*
dejar la barba más larga *keep my beard long*
marcar la línea de la barba *line up my beard*
recortar el bigote *trim my mustache*
rasurar las mejillas y el cuello *shave my cheeks and neck*

Cut types:

un degradado .... *a fade (**puede ser** low fade, mid fade **o** high fade **según la altura del degradado**)*

un rapado .... *a buzz cut*

un corte clásico .... *a classic cut*

un corte militar .... *a crew cut*

un corte con laterales rapados
   y la parte superior larga .... *an undercut*

un corte con textura arriba .... *a textured top*

un corte con raya a un lado .... *a side part haircut*

solo un recorte .... *just a trim*

Facial hair types:

barba

bigote

perilla

patillas

In Spain, we love beards —so much so that we even have expressions like the one below:

Cuando veas a tu vecino las barbas cortar, pon las tuyas a remojar.
When you see your neighbor shaving his beard, soak your own.

Meaning: learn form others misfortunes and take precautions.

I know. Weird.

LET'S GET IN SHAPE

I want to get in shape.

 Let's go to the gym!

Sport is super important. Staying fit is one of the ways we take care of our body and health. Imagine you join the gym and have to face your first session with your personal trainer, but… he doesn't speak English! What do you say? How do you do the exercises he asks you to do? And how do you grab the right tools? Don't worry, **tu amiga Vicky** is here to the rescue, ready to help you and provide the solutions to your problems.

Entrenar: to train

hacer estiramientos *stretching*
hacer sentadillas *squats*
hacer flexiones *push-ups*
hacer la plancha *hold a plank*

hacer abdominales *sit-ups / do crunches*
hacer pesas *lift weights*
hacer dominadas *pull-ups*

Material del gimnasio: gym basics

mancuernas *dumbbells*
pesas *weights*
barra *barbell*
discos *weight plates*
banco de pesas *weight bench*
elíptica *elliptical machine*
bicicleta estática *stationary bike*
cuerda para saltar *jump rope*

kettlebell *kettlebell* (se usa igual en inglés)
pelota *ball*
esterilla *yoga mat*
banda elástica *resistance band*
máquina de pesas *weight machine*
cinta de correr *running belt or treadmill*

USEFUL SENTENCES AT THE GYM

Quiero apuntarme al gimnasio.
I want to sign up for the gym.

Quiero dar de alta/baja este servicio.
I want to activate/cancel this service.

¿Cuánto cuesta la cuota mensual?
How much is the monthly fee?

¿Qué actividades dirigidas están incluidas?
What group classes are included?

¿Tengo acceso a la sala de máquinas?
Do I have access to the gym floor?

¿El entrenador personal se paga aparte?
Does the personal trainer cost extra?

¿Hay piscina, sauna y jacuzzi?
Do you have a pool, sauna and jacuzzi?

¿Tengo que pagar matrícula?
Do I have to pay a registration fee?

Voy al gimnasio para:

bajar de peso / perder peso / adelgazar *lose weight*

subir de peso / engordar *gain weight*

ganar masa muscular *gain muscle mass*

perder grasa *lose fat*

tener más flexibilidad *gain more flexibility*

fortalecer la espalda *strengthen my back*

tonificar mi abdomen *tone my abdomen*

mejorar mi postura *improve my posture*

No, actually I go to the gym to:

descansar de mis hijos
take a break from my kids

IT'S ALL ABOUT SELFCARE

Now, tell me: Which of these activities do you do to take care of yourself? **¿Cuáles de estas actividades haces para cuidarte?**

hacer ejercicio *exercise* ☐

practicar yoga *practice yoga* ☐

meditar *meditate* ☐

comer sano *eat healthy* ☐

dormir bien *sleep well* ☐

beber suficiente agua *drink enough water* ☐

escribir en un diario *write in a journal* ☐

realizar ejercicios de respiración *do breathing exercises* ☐

practicar la gratitud *practice gratitude* ☐

ir al psicólogo *go to a therapist* ☐

bailar *dance* ☐

leer libros de autoayuda *read self-help books* ☐

llevar un estilo de vida organizado *maintain an organized lifestyle* ☐

conectar con la naturaleza *connect with nature* ☐

Otras cosas que haces tú:

____

____

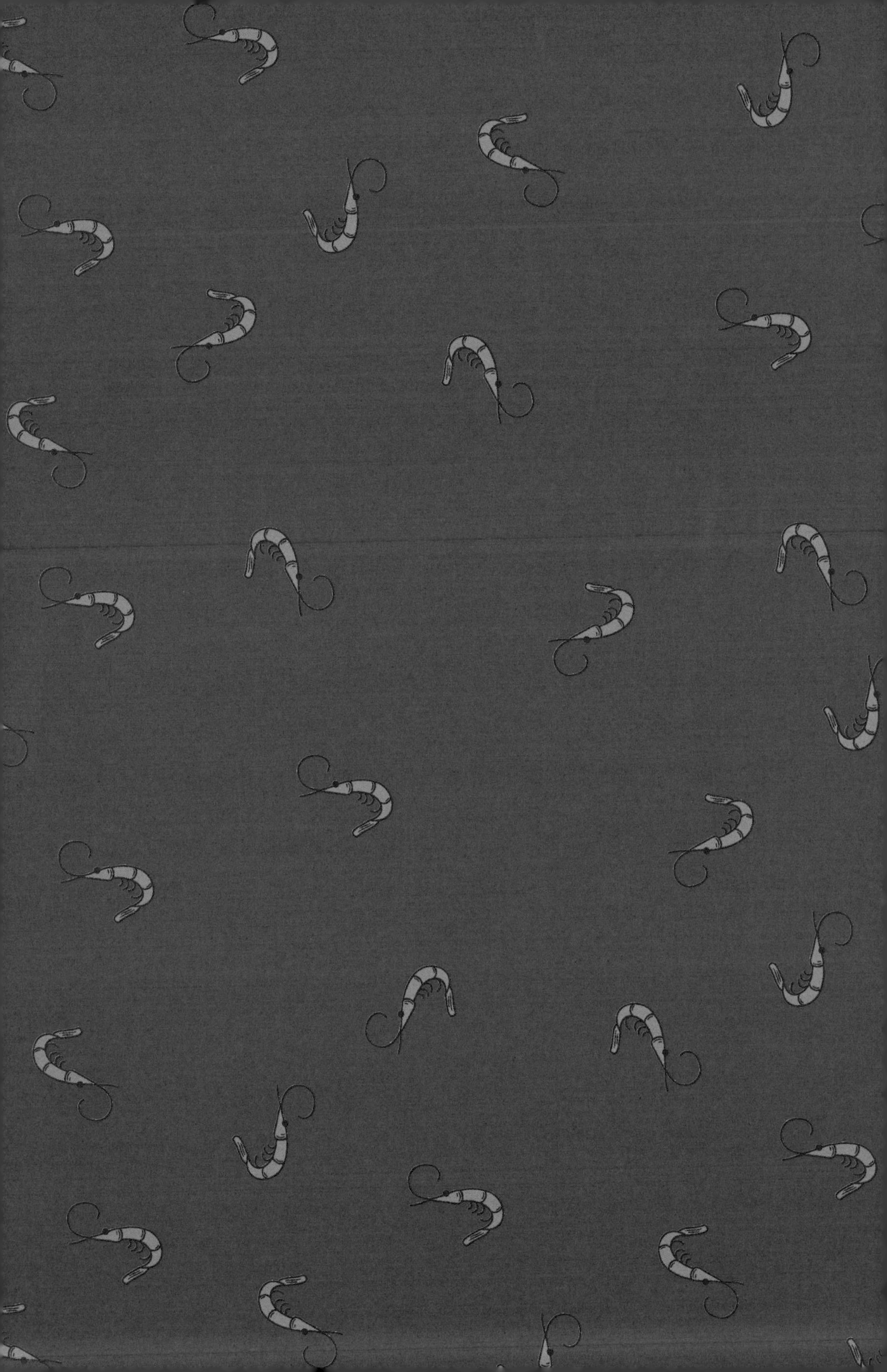

13

MI CASA ES UN DESASTRE

→ Vocabulary basics: at home

→ How to describe house issues

→ Fixing things at home

→ Sorry, I didn't do it on purpose

VOCABULARY BASICS: AT HOME

You've just moved to Spain and still don't feel confident with the language. You arrive at your new apartment and find the kitchen faucet leaking, the living room walls dirty, and you share the flat with two cockroaches. I'm sure you'd like to be able to talk to your landlord and solve all these problems, right? Below, you'll find basic vocabulary related to the house: rooms, pieces of furniture, and some useful phrases.

Confusing words related to house vocabulary:

lavabo
sink in the bathroom

fregadero
sink in the kitchen

uña
nail part of your body

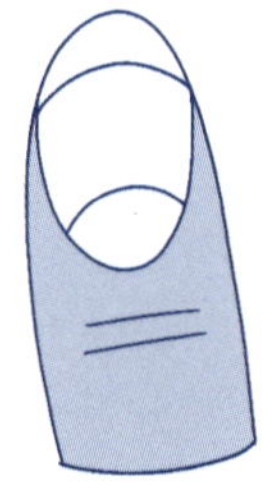

clavo
nail for the wall

almohada
pillow

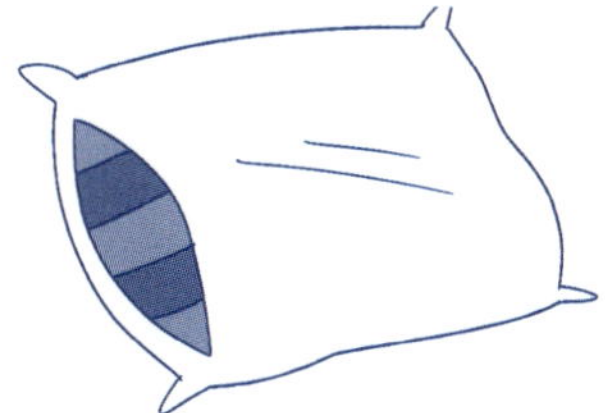

cojín
cushion

techo
ceiling

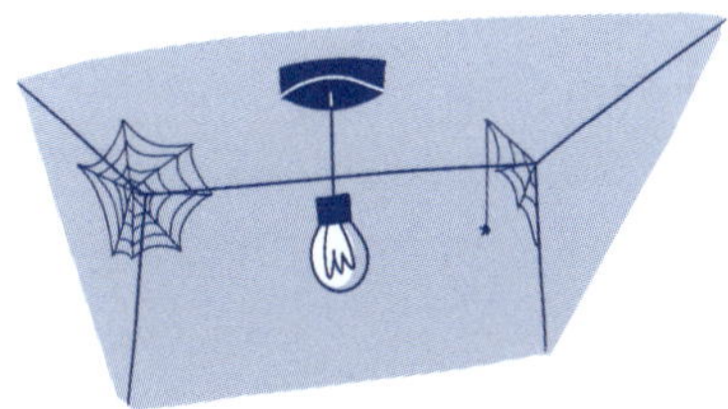

tejado
roof

cerradura
lock in the door

candado
padlock

pilas
batteries

batería
battery

HOW TO DESCRIBE HOUSE ISSUES

I have something to confess.
My worst nightmare
are the **CUCARACHAS**.
Unfortunately, in Spanish
cities in summer, it is very
common to have them
at home. They love heat,
humidity and water.
Every summer, they
visit my house:

**mi peor
pesadilla**
*my worst
nightmare*

CULTURAL TIP

Have you heard the song "**La cucaracha**"?
This is almost a national antem in Spain!

*La cucaracha, la cucaracha, ya no puede caminar
porque no tiene, porque le faltan
las dos patitas de atrás.*

*The cockroach, the cockroach, it can't walk
anymore, because it's missing, because it doesn't
have two hind legs.*

Very common problems that you may have at home (apart from **cucarachas**)

El **váter** está atascado. *The toilet is clogged.*

La **cisterna** pierde agua. *The toilet tank is leaking water.*

La **bombilla** está fundida. *The light bulb is burnt out.*

Se ha quemado el **enchufe**. *The plug has burned out.*

El **grifo** gotea. *The faucet is dripping.*

Ha salido **moho** en la pared. *There is mold on the wall.*

El **radiador** pierde agua. *The radiator is leaking water.*

Hay una **gotera** en el techo. *There's a leak in the ceiling.*

La nevera no **enfría**. *The fridge isn't cooling.*

La puerta **no cierra** bien. *The door doesn't close properly.*

El **aire acondicionado** no funciona. *The air conditioner isn't working.*

Hay una **fuga** de gas. *There's a gas leak.*

La **calefacción** no se enciende. *The heating system won't turn on.*

El **calentador** no funciona. *The hot water isn't working.*

When something doesn't work

How would you say it?

TRABAJAR
No trabaja.
for people

FUNCIONAR
No funciona.
for things and situations

FLUENCY FIX!

When you refer to objects you can also say:
No va. (El mando a distancia no va.)

More useful verbs:

romperse *to break*

estropearse *to get damaged / to break down*

averiarse *to malfunction / to break down*

fundirse *to melt / to burn out (for bulbs, fuses, etc.)*

quemarse *to burn / to get burned*

pincharse *to get a flat tire / to pop (for balloons, tires, etc.)*

mojarse *to get wet*

derramarse *to spill*

FIXING THINGS AT HOME

Fixing the small broken things around the house with your own hands is an incredible feeling. You feel like the most powerful person in the world. But to do it, you need to know some Spanish (oh, surprise). Imagine going to the hardware store and not knowing how to tell the salesperson what you need. Below, you'll find vocabulary related to the small repairs we all like to make at home.

But don't worry. I'm handy. I can fix anything.

- **montar un mueble** *to assemble a piece of furniture*
- **poner un cuadro en la pared** *to hang a picture on the wall*
- **cambiar una bombilla** *to change a light bulb*
- **desatascar el váter / el inodoro** *to unclog the toilet*
- **instalar un ventilador** *to install a fan*
- **cambiar una cerradura** *to change a lock*
- **pintar las paredes** *to paint the walls*
- **tapar agujeros** *to fill in holes*
- **reparar un grifo que gotea** *to fix a leaking faucet*

Here are the tools you can use to repair things at home:

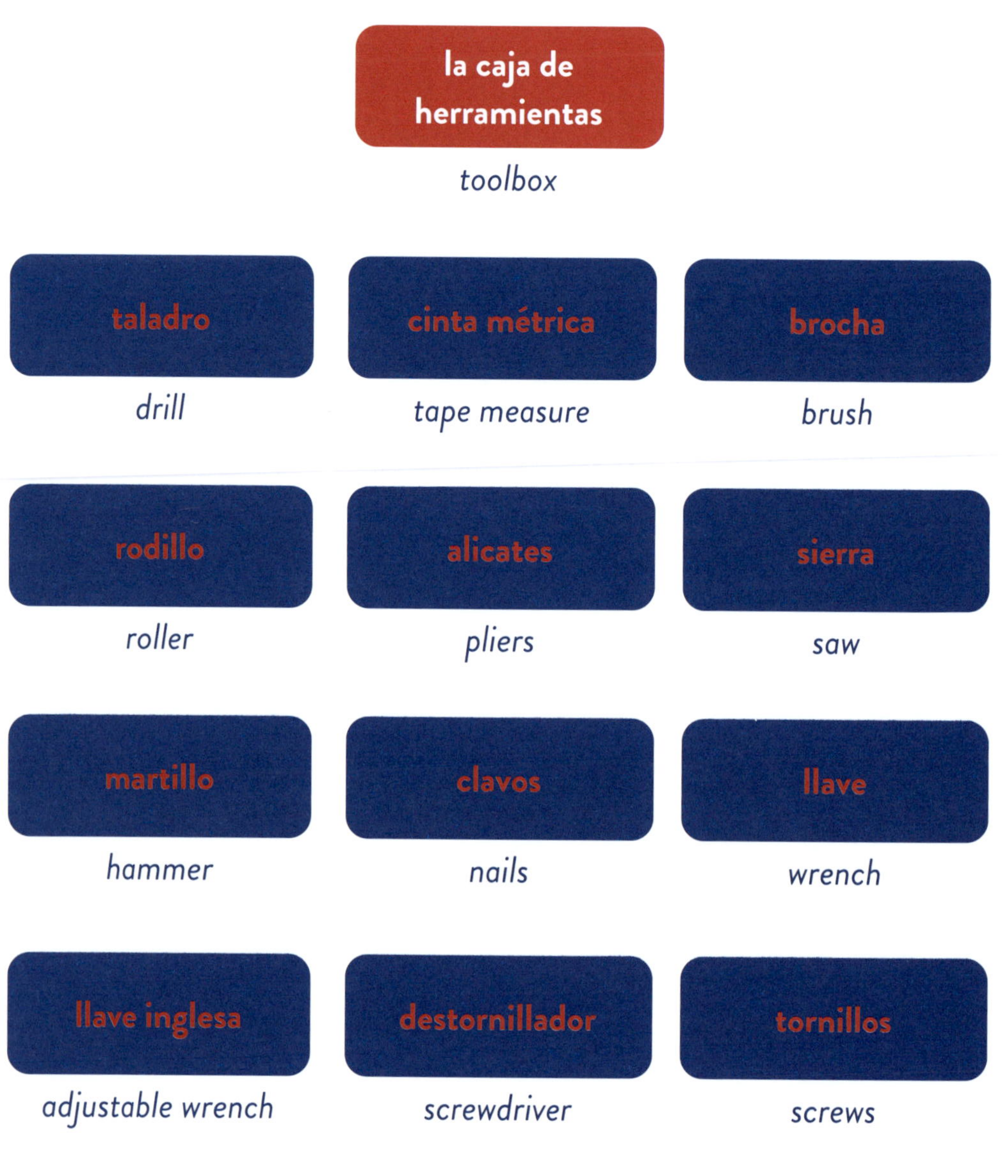

toolbox

drill

tape measure

brush

roller

pliers

saw

hammer

nails

wrench

adjustable wrench

screwdriver

screws

All that being said, don't worry if you are not a handy person (**manitas**), as you can always call a professional. But you must know their names first. Write the names of the professionals related to every object:

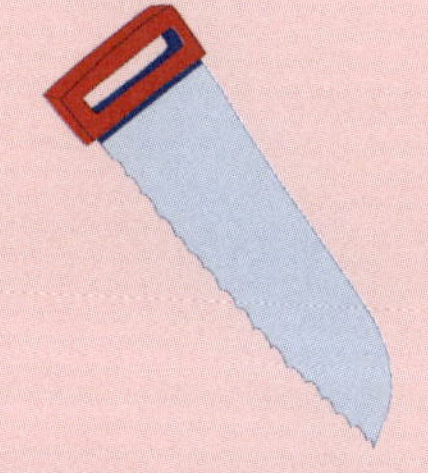  

  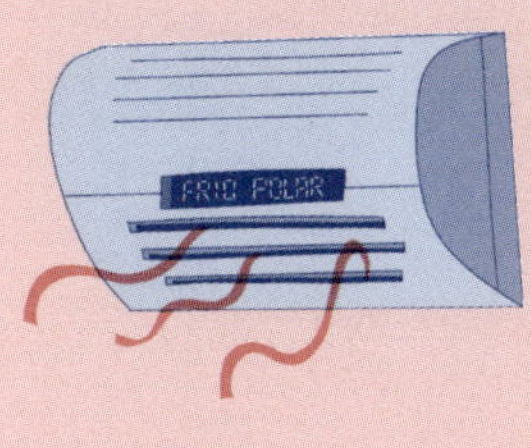

Soluciones:
electricista
carpintero
fontanero

bombero
mecánico
cerrajero

técnico de aire acondicionado
albañil
exterminador de plagas

SORRY, I DIDN'T DO IT ON PURPOSE

As you can see, anything can happen at home. But don't feel guilty about it —we can't always control everything. There are times when, without meaning to, we cause more than one disaster.

I am very clumsy.

También soy un/una manazas, no puedo arreglar nada.

I have two left thumbs and I can't fix anything.

Se me cae todo. *I drop everything.*
Se me olvidan las cosas. *I forget things.*
Se me queman las tostadas. *I burn toast.*
Se me rompe todo. *Everything breaks on me.*

COMMON MISTAKE:
These two are not the same:

¡Ten cuidado! *Be careful!*
Cuídate. *Take care of yourself.*

Voluntary and involuntary actions

Do you know why I use **se me** all the time? Look at this difference:

ACCIÓN VOLUNTARIA
I did it on purpose.
Lo hice a propósito.

ACCIÓN INVOLUNTARIA
I didn't do it on purpose.
Lo hice sin querer.

He roto el cristal.
I broke the glass on purpose.

Se ha roto el cristal.
The glass broke.
(I don't know what happened.)

Se me ha roto el cristal.
The glass broke on me.
(I know what happened: it was an accident.)

GRAMMAR TIP

When we have accidents with objects, we use this grammar structure to emphasize that it wasn't on purpose:

$$\text{SE} \begin{cases} \text{ME} \\ \text{TE} \\ \text{LE} \\ \text{NOS} \\ \text{OS} \\ \text{LES} \end{cases} + \text{VERBO} + \text{SUJETO}$$

You can conjugate the verb in any tense. Here are some examples:

Presente simple: **Siempre se me queman las tostadas.**
Present simple: *I always burn toast.*

Pretérito perfecto: **Esta mañana se te han quemado las tostadas.**
Present perfect: *This morning, you burnt the toast.*

Pretérito indefinido: **Ayer se os quemaron las tostadas.**
Past simple: *Yesterday, you burnt the toast.*

Pretérito imperfecto: **Cuando era niña siempre se le quemaban las tostadas.**
Imperfect: *When she was a child, she always burnt the toast.*

14

DE VIAJE

→ Before exploring new places

→ Different ways to travel

→ Great! You have reached your destination

→ Spain vs **Lationamérica**: confusing words and misunderstandings

BEFORE EXPLORING NEW PLACES

I'm sure you love traveling just as much as I do. I'm an enthusiastic traveler and I can't wait for my next trip. And how would do you say "I can't wait" in Spanish?

Well, this is a literal translation and in Spanish it might sound a bit impatient or negative. If you want to sound more positive, say:

Tengo muchas ganas.
Me muero de ganas.
No veo el momento.
No veo la hora. (old-school expression)

I am always very excited to discover new places. Wait, did you just say **estoy excitada**? Be careful, that means *I'm horny*. This is how we say it:

Estoy muy...
emocionado/a
entusiasmado/a
or, even better: **Me hace mucha ilusión.**

Me hace mucha ilusión conocer España por primera vez.
I'm very excited to get to know Spain for the first time.

¡Saber o conocer?

Saber and **conocer** both mean "to know." Here is the difference:

SABER in these situations:
- **Saber** + noun (facts, information)
- **Saber** + infinitive (how to do something)

Sé la respuesta. *I know the answer.* (fact)

¿**Sabes** dónde está la estación? *Do you know where the station is?* (information)

Sé hablar español. *I know how to speak Spanish.* (skill)

CONOCER in these situations:
- Knowing people (being familiar with someone)
- Being familiar with places
- Being familiar with things (like books, movies, concepts)

GRAMMAR TIP

Conocer ✚ a ✚ person
Conozco a María. *I know María.* (a person)

Conocer ✚ place or thing
¿Conoces Madrid?
Do you know Madrid? (a place)

Conozco esta canción.
I know this song. (familiarity with something)

DIFFERENT WAYS TO TRAVEL

Travelling is an incredible experience. Being able to explore the different and amazing places in the new country you're in can be truly unique. But it's even better if you know how to get around and master the basics of the language. Imagine taking a train or renting a car without knowing any Spanish. What a nightmare, right? Luckily, you have me to help explain some of the key vocabulary for travelling with different types of transport. Come on! Get in the car!

Travelling by car

I have to say that even though I've had my driving license (**carné de conducir**) since I was 18, I don't like driving. **No me gusta conducir.**

> In Spain, we say **conducir**.

> In Latinoamerica it is more common to say **manejar**.

Also, the word **coche** can be different. In Spain, we say **coche**, but according to the country, they might say **carro** or **auto**.

Especially when things like this happen:

Se me ha pinchado una rueda.
A tire has gone flat.

¿Te gusta conducir?

Sí

No

Las partes del coche:

motor *engine*

volante *steering wheel*

asiento *seat*

cinturón de seguridad *seatbelt*

ventanilla *window*

parabrisas *windshield*

retrovisor *rearview mirror*

faros *headlights*

freno *brake*

acelerador *accelerator*

embrague *clutch*

rueda *wheel*

llantas *rims*

neumáticos *tires*

maletero *trunk*

bocina *horn*

batería *battery*

radiador *radiator*

More verbs that you will need if you drive a car:

arrancar el coche *to start the car*

frenar *to brake*

acelerar *to accelerate*

poner marcha atrás *to go in reverse*

aparcar/estacionar *to park*

cambiar de marcha *to shift gears*

encender las luces *to turn on the lights*

poner el intermitente *to turn on the turn signal/indicator*

revisar el aceite *to check the oil*

poner gasolina *to fill the gas tank*

poner el freno de mano *to pull the handbrake / parking brake*

Travelling by train

I love traveling by train.
Me encanta viajar en tren.

Let's learn some useful sentences that you are going to use at the train station (**en la estación de tren**):

Quería un billete de ida y vuelta.
I'd like a round-trip ticket.
¿Este billete es válido para cualquier tren?
Is this ticket valid for any train?
¿A qué hora sale el próximo tren?
What time does the next train leave?
¿Este tren va a Barcelona?
Does this train go to Barcelona?
¿De qué andén sale el tren?
Which platform does the train leave from?
¿Este es un tren directo o hay que hacer transbordo?
Is this a direct train or do I need to transfer?
¿Cuánto tarda el tren en llegar?
How long does the train take to get there?

GRAMMAR TIP

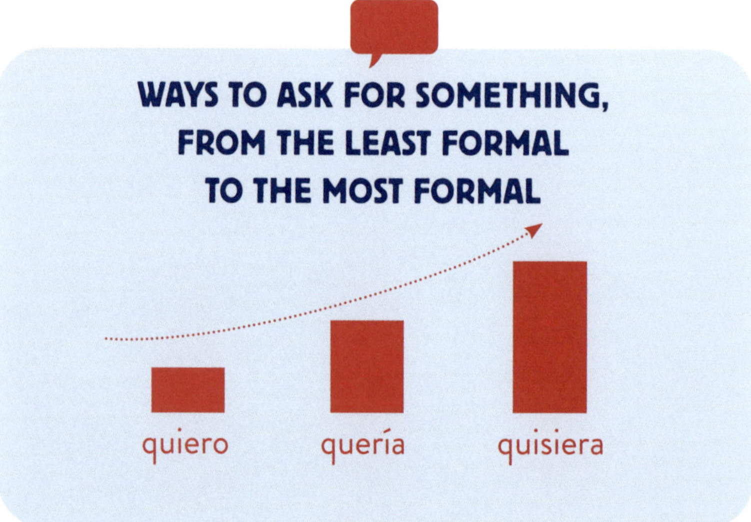

Sentences that you need inside the train:

¿Está ocupado este asiento? *Is this seat taken?*
¿Dónde puedo poner mi maleta? *Where can I put my suitcase?*
¿Cuál es la próxima parada? *What's the next stop?*
Creo que este es mi asiento. *I think this is my seat.*
Me bajo en la próxima parada. *I get off at the next stop.*
Mi tren va con retraso. *My train is delayed.*

Travelling by plane

vuelo *flight*
pasaporte *passport*
billete (used in Spain) **/ boleto** (used in Latin America) *ticket*
mostrador de facturación *check-in counter*
equipaje facturado *check-in luggage*
tarjeta de embarque *boarding pass*
puerta de embarque *boarding gate*
control de seguridad *security checkpoint*
sala de espera *waiting room*
aerolínea *airline*
equipaje de mano *carry-on luggage*

maleta *suitcase*
retiro de equipaje *baggage claim*
control de pasaportes *passport control*
retraso *delay*
hora de salida *departure time*
hora de llegada *arrival time*
maletero *baggage handler*
ventanilla de información *information desk*
aterrizaje *landing*
despegue *takeoff*
terminal *terminal*
cinturón de seguridad *seatbelt*
zona de aduanas *customs area*

GREAT! YOU HAVE REACHED YOUR DESTINATION

After a short or long trip, you've finally arrived at your destination. Time to explore!

Useful sentences when you arrive at the hotel:

Tengo una reserva a nombre de... *I have a reservation under the name...*

¿A qué hora es el check-out? *What time is check-out?*

¿Cuál es la clave del wifi? *What's the Wi-Fi password?*

¿A qué hora se sirve el desayuno? *What time is breakfast served?*

¿Me puede dar más toallas? *Can you give me more towels?*

¿Hay servicio de habitaciones? *Is there room service?*

¿Tienen caja fuerte en la habitación? *Do you have a safe in the room?*

¿Puedo hacer el check-in antes? *Can I check in earlier?*

¿Hay algún cargo adicional? *Is there any additional charge?*

¿Puedo dejar mi equipaje aquí después del check-out? *Can I leave my luggage here after check-out?*

Finally, you arrived at the city but...

Está a punto de llover. *It's about to rain* 😔

Espera, voy a coger un paraguas, por si las moscas.
Wait, I'm going to grab an umbrella,

FLUENCY FIX!

por si las moscas *just in case*

Okay, this is a weird expression. I know.
You can also say: por si acaso 😉

POR VS PARA

Let's look at the most confusing prepositions in Spanish:

Voy **por la ciudad**.
I walk in the city.

Voy **para la ciudad**.
I go to the city. (like a or hacia)

Miro **por** la ventana.
I look out the window.

Miro **para** la ventana.
I look to the window.

Estudio español **por** mi marido.
*I study Spanish because
of my husband.*

Estudio español **para** hablar
con mi marido.
*I study Spanish to speak
with my husband.*

Lo hago **por** ti.
I do it instead of you. / I do it because of you.

Lo hago **para** ti.
I do it for you.
(you are the final goal)

Lo hago **por la mañana**.
I do it in the morning.

Lo hago (hoy) **para mañana**.
I'm doing it for tomorrow.

GRAMMAR TIP

As you can see in the examples above, you can't translate these prepositions literally into English, but you can try to visualize the movement:

POR  **PARA**

The best way to think about **por** is as a movement that goes around or through the action and indicates the reason.

The best way to think about **para** is as a straight and forward movement in space or time.

How to ask for and give directions

¿Sabes dónde hay una farmacia por aquí cerca?
Do you know where there's a pharmacy nearby?
¿Cómo puedo ir a...?
How can I get to...?
Gira a la derecha.
Turn right.
Gira a la izquierda.
Turn left.
Continúa todo recto.
Go straight ahead / Keep going straight.
Está delante de...
It's in front of...
Está detrás de...
It's behind...
Está al lado de...
It's next to... / Beside...
Está cerca de...
It's near... / Close to...
Está lejos de...
It's far from...
Está a la vuelta de la esquina.
It's around the corner.
Está al final de la calle.
At the end of the street.

No tiene pérdida.
You can't miss it.
¿Está cerca o necesito coger un taxi?
Is it close, or do I need to take a taxi?
¿Cuánto se tarda en llegar andando?
How long does it take to get there on foot?
Creo que me he perdido.
I think I'm lost.

TARDAR VS DURAR

TARDAR = *To take (time to do something)*

TARDAR + AMOUNT OF TIME + **EN** + INFINITIVE

El tren tardará dos horas en llegar.
The train will take two hours to arrive.

DURAR = *To last (duration of something)*
Use **durar** when talking about how long something lasts.

DURAR + AMOUNT OF TIME

¿Cuánto dura el curso? *How long does the course last?*

In summary:

Tardar:
How long it takes to do something.
It takes me...

Durar:
How long something lasts.
The movie lasts...

SPAIN VS LATINOAMÉRICA: CONFUSING WORDS AND MISUNDERSTANDINGS

To end this chapter, I want to talk about some funny misunderstandings that I had with my Latino friends. You must know these things if you travel in Spanish-speaking countries.

> The day I argued about the color of a **LIMÓN** with my Mexican friend.

In Spain, the **limón** is yellow. We don't have green lemons, we have **limes**: **limas**. In Mexico, **lemons are green**.

> The day I said voy a **COGER** la botella to my **Argentine** friend.

Coger means "**to take**" in Spain. In other countries, they say **agarrar**. **Coger** means "**to have sex**" in most Spanish-speaking countries.

> The day I said my aunt's name was **CONCHA** to my **Uruguayan** friend.

Concha is a very common woman's name in Spain. **Concha** is the vagina in some countries like **Argentina** and **Uruguay**.

Have you ever experienced any of these misunderstandings?

15

VISITA MÉDICA

- → Doctor, ¿qué me pasa?
- → How to describe your symptoms
- → Specific health issues
- → At the pharmacy

DOCTOR, ¿QUÉ ME PASA?

Diagnosis: Spanish is giving you a headache.
El español te da dolor de cabeza.

Now let's correct the mistakes:

***No comprendo.** If you want to sound more natural use this:

✔ No lo entiendo.
✔ Perdona, ¿qué has dicho?
✔ ¿Cómo dices?

or just ➤ ✔ ¿Cómo?

Also, it is not rude to say **¿Qué?** in Spanish like in English: "What?"

***No problema.** This is an incorrect way to say "**No problem.**"

You must say:
- ✔ **No hay problema.**
- ✔ **Sin problema.**
- ✔ **Ningún problema.**

And if you want to sound more like a native, say:
- ✔ **No pasa nada.**
- ✔ **No te preocupes.**
- ✔ **Tranquilo/a.** (or just **tranqui**)

***No me recuerdo.** This is also incorrect.

We say:
- ✔ **No me acuerdo.**
- ✔ **No lo recuerdo.**

You can use the verbs **acordarse** de algo or **recordar** algo.

***Soy un profesor.** Don't use the indefinite article when referring to your profession. Simply say:
- ✔ **Soy profesora, soy enfermero…**

***Me duele mi cabeza.** Don't use the pronoun **mi** when you use **me**. It's not necessary, because we already know that it's your head.

Use the definite article instead:
- ✔ Me duele **la** cabeza.

***Un solución.** **Solución** is always a feminine noun. In Spanish, all nouns ending in **-ción** or **-sión** are feminine.
- ✔ Necesito **una** solución.

HOW TO DESCRIBE YOUR SYPMTOMS

ESTOY + ADJECTIVE
resfriado/a *I have a cold.*
mareado/a *I feel dizzy.*

We are describing circumstance

When we talk about an illness.

SOY + ADJECTIVE
alérgico/a *I am allergic to...*
diabético/a *I am diabetic.*
asmático/a *I am asthmatic.*
hipertenso/a *I have high blood pressure.*

TENGO + NOUN
I have:

diarrea *diarrhea*
fiebre *fever*
tos *a cough*
gripe *the flu*
insomnio *insomnia*
ansiedad *anxiety*

depresión *depression*
dolor muscular *muscle pain*
una herida *a wound*
un hematoma *a bruise*
un bulto *a lump*

We don't use the definite or indefinite articles

COMMON MISTAKE: Wait, did you just say that you are constipated? Thank you, but I don't need that information.

In Spain, **estoy constipado/a** means **I have a cold**, but in other Spanish-speaking countries, like Argentina, it means **I'm constipated**, like in English. In Spain, when we are constipated, we say this:

estoy estreñido

Other symptoms:

- **Me pican los ojos.** *My eyes itch.*
- **Me sudan las manos.** *My hands are sweaty.*
- **Me cuesta respirar.** *I have trouble breathing.*
- **Se me seca la boca.** *My mouth is dry.*

Explain what happened to you:

Me ha picado una medusa / una abeja.
I was stung by a jellyfish / a bee.
Me ha mordido un perro.
I got bitten by a dog.
Me he dado un golpe.
I got hit / I took a blow.
Me he torcido el tobillo.
I twisted my ankle.
Me he cortado el dedo.
I cut my finger.
Me he hecho sangre.
I drew blood.
Me he caído.
I fell.
He resbalado.
I slipped.
He tropezado.
I tripped.

¡Y A TI QUÉ TE DUELE?

Cuéntame algún problema de salud que hayas tenido y qué síntomas sentiste. Tell me about a health problem you've had and what symptoms you felt.

SPECIFIC HEALTH ISSUES

All of the above is very good and super useful, but what happens when we have a specific health issue? Let's dive in.

The period

Fellow menstruators, here you have some ways to say **"I am on my period"**:

> **TENGO LA REGLA.**
> Me ha venido la regla.
> Me ha bajado la regla.
> Estoy con la regla.
> Tengo la menstruación. (formal)
> Tengo el periodo. (formal)

Necesito...

un tampón *a tampon*
una compresa *a sanitary pad*
un salvaslip *a panty liner*
una copa menstrual *a menstrual cup*
una braguita menstrual *a period panty*
un ibuprofeno *an ibuprofen*

> **TENGO UN RETRASO.**
> *I'm late (for my period).*

¡O una copa!

Necesito...
un test de embarazo
a pregnancy test

Let's go to the dentist:

Tengo una caries. *I have a cavity.*

Tengo un empaste. *I have a filling.*

Me han quitado las muelas del juicio. *I got my wisdom teeth pulled.*

Me han puesto carillas. *I got veneers put on.*

Tengo sarro. *I have tartar.*

Llevo aparatos. *I wear braces.*

Necesito una férula para dormir. *I need a night guard.*

Me voy a hacer una limpieza dental. *I'm going to get my teeth cleaned.*

Me sangran las encías. *My gums are bleeding.*

Me he roto un diente. *I broke a tooth.*

Llevo dentadura postiza. *I wear dentures.*

Me han puesto un implante dental. *I got a dental implant.*

Necesito llevar retenedores. *I need to wear retainers.*

Llevo alineadores invisibles. *I wear invisible aligners.*

At the eye doctor

Yes, this literally means "I don't see three people on a donkey."
I can't see a thing

Tengo miopía. *I am nearsighted. / I have myopia.*

Tengo astigmatismo. *I have astigmatism.*

Tengo hipermetropía. *I am farsighted. / I have hyperopia.*

Llevo lentillas. *I wear contact lenses.*

Necesito gafas. *I need glasses.*

No veo de cerca. *I can't see up close.*

No veo de lejos. *I can't see far away.*

Tengo vista cansada. *I have presbyopia. / I have tired eyes.*

Se me secan los ojos. *My eyes get dry.*

Veo borroso. *My vision is blurry.*

Tengo cataratas. *I have cataracts.*

AT THE PHARMACY

Now that you have a diagnosis of what's going on, it's time to go to the pharmacy so they can give you the appropriate medication. Let's see how you can ask for it in Spanish:

medicamentos *medicine*	**pastillas** *pills*	**jarabe** *syrup*	**pomada** *ointment*
crema *cream*	**cápsulas** *capsules*	**analgésicos** *painkillers*	**antiinflamatorios** *anti-inflammatories*
antibióticos *antibiotics*	**termómetro** *thermometer*	**tiritas** *band-aids*	**vendas** *bandages*
gotas para los ojos *eyedrops*	**pastillas para la garganta** *throat lozenges*	**espray nasal** *nasal spray*	**chicles de nicotina** *nicotine gum*
lentes de contacto / lentillas *contact lenses*	**pasta de dientes** *toothpaste*	**cepillo de dientes** *toothbrush*	**desodorante** *deodorant*
	hilo dental *dental floss*	**crema hidratante** *moisturizer*	

WELL, WE HAVE REACHED THE END. AND IN CASE THIS BOOK DIDN'T CURE YOUR "SPANISH ACHE" ENTIRELY, I'M GOING TO OFFER YOU A MAGIC PILL.

As we say in Spanish:

A grandes males, grandes remedios.
Desperate times call for desperate measures.

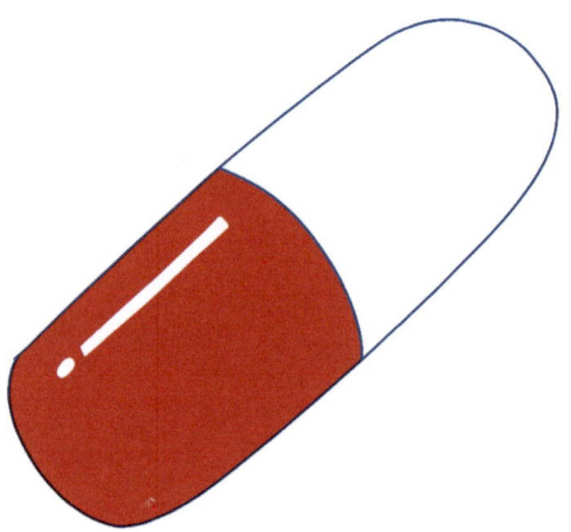

TENER ACENTO NATIVO
Having a native accent

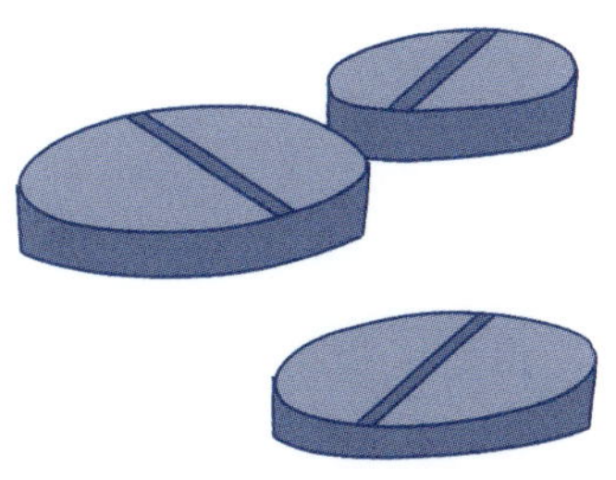

DOMINAR POR Y PARA

Mastering por and para

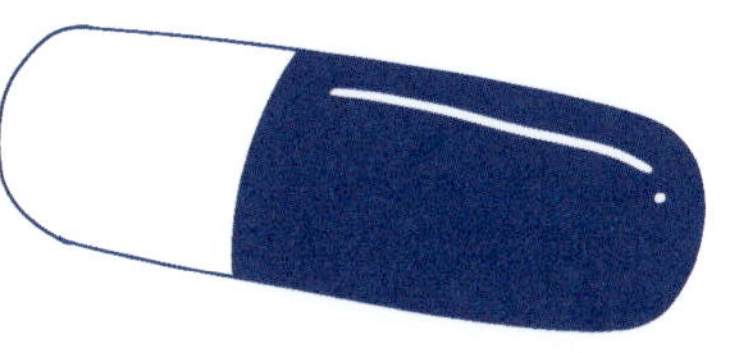

ENTENDER A LOS NATIVOS

Understanding native speakers

HABLAR CON FLUIDEZ

Speaking fluently

DOMINAR EL SUBJUNTIVO

Mastering the subjunctive

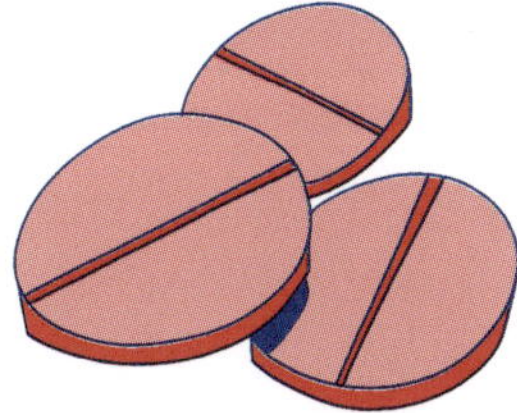

RECORDAR TODO EL VOCABULARIO

Remembering all the vocabulary

NOW TELL ME: WHICH ONE WOULD YOU TAKE? 😉

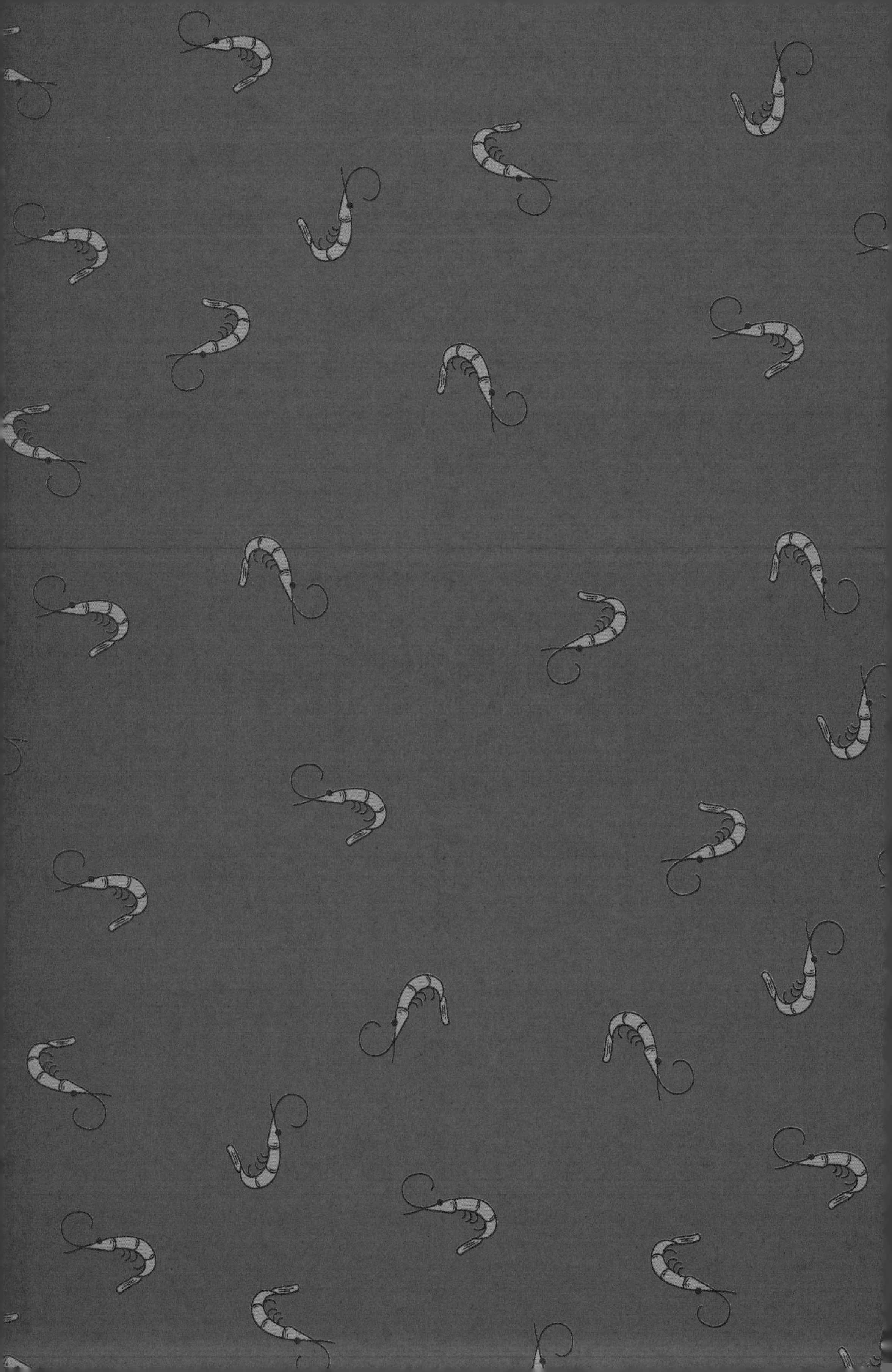

YOU CAN SPEAK SPANISH

Well, it seems we've reached the end of this journey together, but really, this is just the beginning for you.

Learning a language is not about perfection —it's about connection. If you've made it this far, you already have the tools to speak Spanish. Now, it's time to let go of the fear, embrace the mistakes, and just speak.

Remember, every fluent speaker was once a beginner. The difference? They kept going. The more you practice, the more confident you'll become. Speak with natives, make mistakes, laugh at yourself, and keep learning. That's how real progress happens.

And don't be afraid —Spanish speakers will love seeing you make the effort. We are a warm, welcoming people, and we truly appreciate it when someone tries to speak our language. Nobody expects perfection, just your willingness to communicate. So don't hold back!

Spanish is not just a language —it's a door to new experiences, friendships, and opportunities. And trust me, you are capable of learning it.

So go out there, speak up, and enjoy the journey.

¡TÚ PUEDES!
¡HASTA PRONTO Y SIGUE PRACTICANDO!

Este libro se terminó de imprimir
en el mes de junio de 2025.

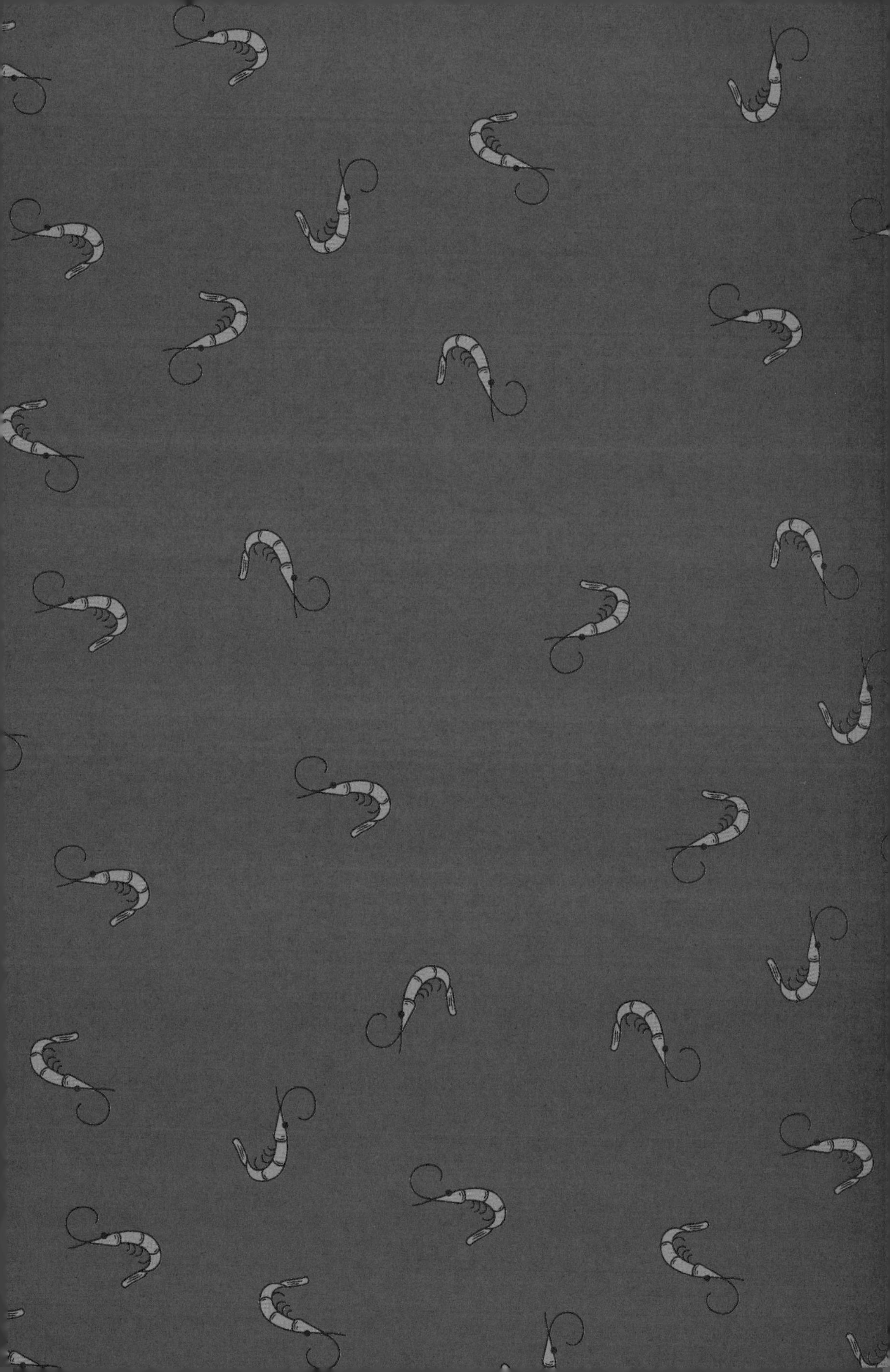

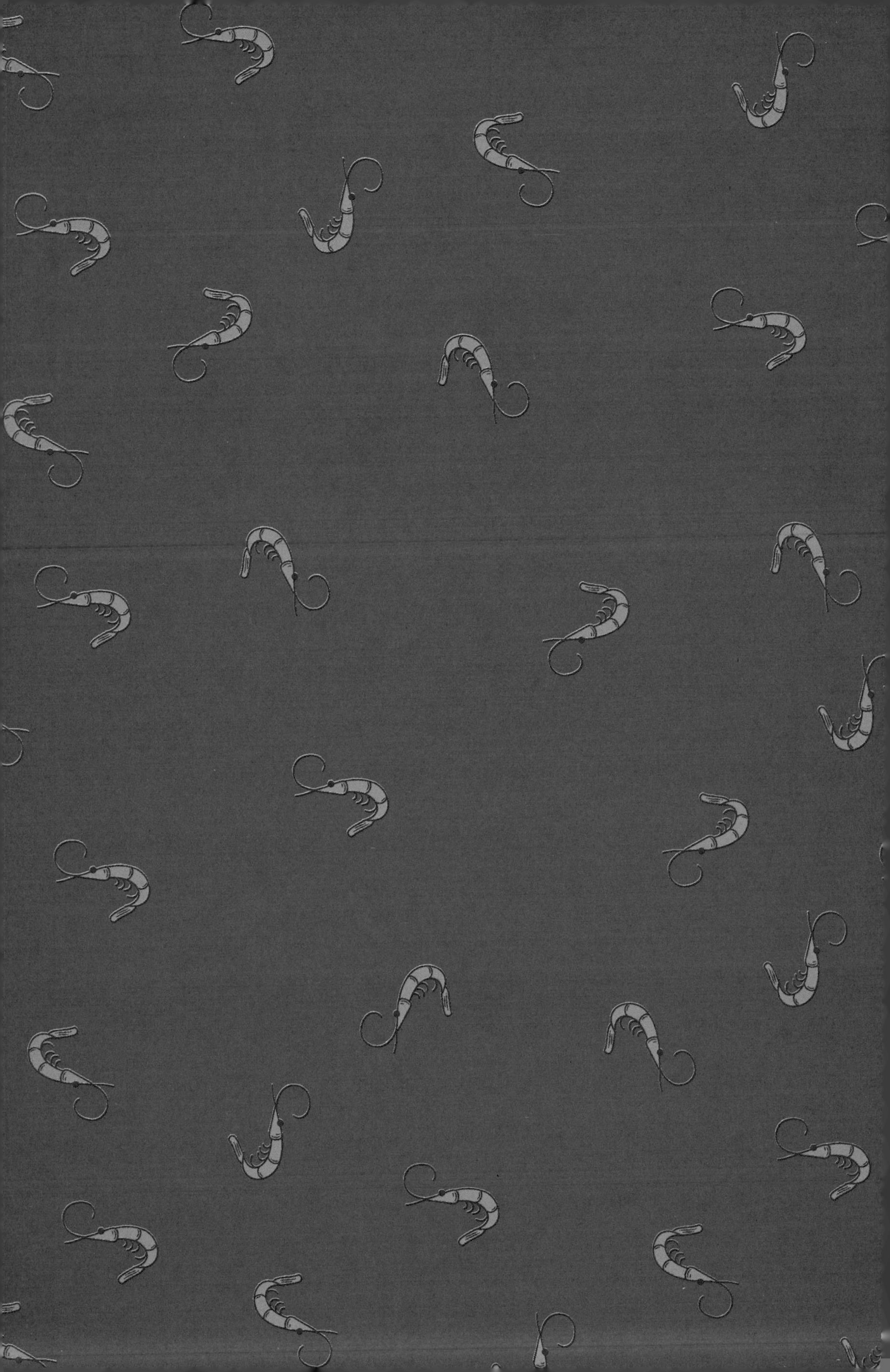